American Society for Training & Develop

Brenda Hubbard

Improving On-the-Job Training and Coaching

- Identify best OJT trainer candidates
- Create super training plans
- Ensure transfer of training
- Learn skillful coaching for peak performance

by Karen Lawson

Foreword by Mel Silberman

To Jeffrey Lawson and Andrew Lawson:
the sources of my most challenging and rewarding
on-the-job training experience.

Ordering information: Books published by the American Society for Training & Development can be ordered by calling 703.683.8100.

Library of Congress Catalog Card Number: 97-73683
ISBN: 1-56286-062-3

 ASTD *Delivering Performance in a Changing World*

1640 King Street
Box 1443
Alexandria, VA 22313-2043
PH 703.683.8100, FX 703.683.8103
www.astd.org

Contents

Foreword

One of my favorite exercises is to cover my wristwatch with my hand and ask those who are observing me: "What am I doing?" Immediately, someone will say: "You're covering your watch." I request a synonym for the word cover. Typically, I hear suggestions such as "hide," obscure," or "block." With this opening, I quip that the next time *you* have something to cover with a person you are training, you might be hiding the information, obscuring it, or completely blocking it from view. That's because, at that moment, it's *your* information and *your* understanding of it. It does not belong to the *other* person. As you cover the subject matter, the other person has to "uncover" what you are saying.

On-the-job training, as Karen Lawson so clearly demonstrates in this gem of a book, is not a casual *telling* of information but a carefully thought out process of helping someone else *take away* the knowledge or skill needed to perform a job. If the trainee is to possess the knowledge or skill, the trainer must supply instruction, guidance, and follow-up support.

Karen Lawson understands better than most people that learning anything, except for things we pretty much know already, is not an automatic consequence of pouring information into another person's head. She respects the learner's frame of reference because she remembers her own frustrations as a learner (as you will read) when faced with a supervisor who thinks that teaching someone a job is a matter of "show and tell" on the one hand or "sink or swim" on the other. Karen believes that merely hearing something and seeing it is not enough to learn it. Learning is an active search for understanding that requires the learner's own efforts. At the same time, she also believes that an on-the-job trainer should not leave the trainee to his or her own devices, but should serve as a coach and a collaborator who provides direction, patience, and partnership.

Most of all, you will discover from your own active reading of *Improving On-the-Job Training and Coaching* that OJT requires a multistep plan of action that is well worth the effort if you truly want to help others perform rather than fail. Karen helps you to be an active reader by including mini exercises to facilitate your improvement as a trainer and coach. After all, she is faced with the same challenge as you are-to train and coach you as you train and coach others. At this task, she does a remarkable job.

Mel Silberman
Active Training
Princeton, New Jersey

Introduction

"I've told them and told them how to do it, and they still do it wrong."

"What's the matter with these people? Can't they follow directions?"

"Today's employees—here today and gone tomorrow. It's like a revolving door around here."

According to a two-year joint study by the American Society for Training and Development (ASTD) and the U.S. Department of Labor, "by the year 2000, there are likely to be too few well-educated and well-trained workers to satisfy the nation's economic needs" (American Society for Training and Development 1988). Although this study relates specifically to the United States, the implication is global. In another study conducted by the American Federation of Teachers and released in July 1995, the union which represents public school teachers and other education workers concluded that "America's schools are doing a poor job of preparing students for the workforce" (Briscoe 1995). A report accompanying that study further states that "the United States currently has the worst school-to-work system in the industrialized world" (Briscoe 1995). For years, employers have recognized the importance of the autonomous employee for efficiency, quality, customer relations, and the development of innovations and new applications for existing products and services. Yet this learning deficit threatens the economic growth of nations throughout the world.

As we move into the 21st century, the three Cs of corporate concern will have even greater impact on our global economy. Competition, composition, and change are the trends shaping the world of the late 1990s and beyond. Increased international competition places greater demands on companies' resources, particularly their *human* resources. A company's competitive edge depends on a skilled workforce but labor shortages are common internationally, especially in the United States. This shrinking pool of workers and the public school system's poor preparation of young people to function in the world of work are forcing companies to reconsider the way they view and use their human resources. Rapid change and increased technology have resulted in novel skill requirements and more complex jobs with fewer qualified people to fill them. Downsizing casualties find themselves displaced and forced to learn new skills in order to meet new employment demands. Companies are under even greater pressure in today's competitive environment to increase productivity and profitability through well-trained employees producing quality products and services.

No Time for Training

Today's flat organizations and lean departments create new challenges for training. Companies are concerned about doing more with less. As a result, they must rely on on-the-job training to bring their employees up to speed. On the average a new worker can spend over 150 hours in on-the-job training (140 hours of which are conducted informally) during the first three months of employment, at a considerable cost to the company (Barron, Black, and Lowenstein 1989). Because companies are expected to do more with fewer people, it is quite likely that on-the-job training will continue to be the principal means by which changes are integrated into the work place. In fact, 82 percent of the organizations responding to the 1995 Industry Report published by *Training* magazine use one-on-one instruction as a primary delivery method, ranking it third behind videotape (82 percent) and lecture (90 percent) (1995).

This book gives managers, supervisors, or other designated trainers a structured process for developing and implementing a comprehensive, efficient, and cost-effective program to train workers on the job to develop new skills, assume new responsibilities, or improve current performance. Its focus is on improving the performance of both the new employee learning a new job and the seasoned employee learning new and different skills. In both cases, the emphasis is on active learner involvement and individual accountability.

In her article titled "Reinventing the Profession" in *Training and Development,* Patricia Galagan reports that "more learning is occurring just-in-time and directly in the context of a job or a task." This book presents such a just-in-time approach and puts the methodology for helping employees acquire knowledge or learn skills in the hands of those "who own performance problems" (Galagan 1994). This book addresses directly the following technical competencies as identified in ASTD's *Models for HRD Practice:* Adult learning understanding, competency identification skill, objectives preparation skill, and training and development theories and techniques understanding (McLagan 1989).

As with all training, the goal of on-the-job training is to improve performance. Such instruction can and does improve workplace performance if it is created and implemented to ensure consistency and uniformity. The tools and techniques presented in this book will help both novices and experienced trainers design and develop an on-the-job training program that will produce bottom-line business results.

About the Author

Karen Lawson, consultant, speaker, and writer, is president of Lawson Consulting Group, a consulting firm specializing in organization and management development. Lawson has extensive consulting and workshop experience in the areas of communication, management, quality service, and team development.

She has a doctorate in Organization Development from Temple University. She earned her M.A. from the University of Akron and B.A. from Mount Union College. She is also a graduate of the National School of Banking in Fairfield, CT.

She was 1992 President of the Philadelphia-Delaware Valley Chapter of the American Society for Training & Development and was Director of the ASTD National Executive Committee of the Sales and Marketing Professional Practice Area. She is currently on the adjunct faculty of the University of Delaware and Villa Nova University.

Karen Lawson may be reached at Lawson Consulting Group, 1365 Gwynedale Way, Lansdale, PA 19446. Phone: 215.368.9465.

Acknowledgments

I would like to thank Robert Maiden of Maxwell Training Centers, Laurie Green of Alliance Bank, Deborah Jacovelli of Commerce Bank, and William Taylor of PECO Energy for their input and suggestions.

As always, I express my appreciation to my mother, Mildred Eells, who taught me some valuable life lessons. Finally, I am especially grateful to my husband and best friend, Bob Lawson, for his technical and moral support as well as his love and understanding.

Chapter 1
Overview of Structured On-the-Job Training

Chapter Objectives:
- Recognize the need for structured on-the-job training
- Define on-the-job training and on-the-job coaching
- Identify situations that require on-the-job training and those that don't

Today's workplace is a rapidly changing environment. Workers must acquire new skills almost daily. Complex technology demands more highly trained workers but there are fewer qualified people to fill the jobs. In addition, there is a decreasing pool of younger workers available. The dilemma: Outplace employees and hire new ones, or retrain existing workers?

Replacing underskilled employees is costly and companies are recognizing that retraining current employees closes the gap between required and available skills and improves performance in both blue-collar and white-collar jobs.

Haphazard or unstructured training methods such as *shadowing,* in which a new employee merely follows an experienced employee, often prove inadequate. At the same time, financial constraints and staffing considerations often preclude sending employees to off-site training programs. Classroom training—even in-house—has a major impact on a department's productivity. These concerns about time, money, and lack of qualified personnel mean that companies have placed a greater emphasis on on-the-job training to shorten the job-related learning cycle, especially where technology is changing rapidly, company sites are geographically widespread, and many people need training. Small companies that employ too few people to warrant a training staff and a formal classroom program are also turning to on-the-job training.

On-the-Job Training and Coaching Defined

On-the-job training traces its origins to ancient times when tradesmen learned their crafts through informal apprenticeship programs with master craftsmen. The term *on-the-job training (OJT)* has several definitions, depending on the researcher or the time period under discussion. Some authorities use the term to include any training, individual or classroom-style, that occurs at the worksite. Others apply it to both structured and unstructured approaches.

Throughout the centuries, educators and psychologists have influenced the development of industrial training methods. A significant outgrowth of their work was the four-step method of job instruction adopted and used extensively by the U.S. military in World War I: Preparation, presentation, application, and inspection. This approach evolved into small-group training programs conducted by supervisors in order to standardize instruction. During World War II, the four-step method was further refined to a seven-step method: Show, explain, observe instructor, practice, assist, observe learner, and perform job independently (McCord 1987). This seven-step method, used primarily to train lens grinders, resulted in a reduction of training time from five years to six months (Jacobs and Jones 1995). Some people, however, found the seven-step approach too cumbersome. As a result, the Job Instruction Training program established in 1940 and discontinued after the war returned to the original four-step method and many organizations, including the federal government, use this approach today.

> **On-the-job training** is a structured process conducted at the employee's workarea to provide the employee with the knowledge and skills to perform job tasks.

> **On-the-job coaching** is an ongoing process designed to help the employee gain greater competence and overcome barriers to improving performance.

For the purposes of this book, on-the-job training is a structured process conducted at the employee's workarea to provide the employee with the knowledge and skills to perform job tasks. OJT is finite; it has a beginning and an end. It is used in training the newly hired, in cross-training, and in retraining current employees.

Most definitions, including the one just offered, don't fit many work environments, and to keep pace with the ever-changing nature of work, training must be regarded as an ongoing process that needs to be refined continually. For that reason, I also include *on-the-job coaching (OJC)* as part of the entire OJT process. In contrast to OJT, on-the-job coaching is an ongoing process designed to help the employee gain greater competence and overcome barriers to improving performance.

Both OJT and OJC are conducted by the employee's supervisor or a designated coworker on a one-on-one (or small-group), nonclassroom basis either in place of or as a supplement to a group classroom training program. Adding the coaching strategy becomes increasingly appropriate as employees become more self-directed and the manager's role becomes that of coach and facilitator.

Little research has been conducted to measure bottom-line results from a structured approach to OJT. One study, however, does support the theory that better results are achieved by such structured training. Rothwell and Kazanas (1990) found that when no structured training was offered, employees generally consulted their coworkers and "procedure" to learn what to do. Without a planned approach, instruction and procedures were not standardized, and trainees often picked up bad practices from their "teachers." This haphazard approach often results in a greater number of errors, lower productivity, and increased employee frustration.

For example, take a bank teller's situation. Let's assume we have two new teller trainees. Each trainee has been assigned a "personal trainer." Because the bank has no formal process for training an employee on the job, the trainers are left to their own devices to determine what should be taught and how. So, what's wrong with that? Trainer A is very thorough, training the new employee "by the book" and taking the extra time needed to reinforce the training and observe the trainee's performance to make sure he's doing everything correctly. Trainer B, on the other hand, is used to taking shortcuts and passes these procedural deviations on to the trainee. Furthermore, B's approach is to tell and show the trainee only once how to do the task and then leave her to try it alone with no further supervision. Not only will the trainee assigned to B feel frustrated and insecure, but the level of service delivered by the two trainees will probably be quite different. This, of course, can have serious consequences, including customer annoyance, dissatisfaction, and perhaps lost business for the bank.

When there is no system the trainee may or may not learn everything that's needed. There is no consistency or uniformity. The trainee will probably learn the trainer's way of doing the job, which may not be correct or may not be appropriate to that particular trainee.

On-the-job training approaches such as "shadow Sally and Sam" (observation and imitation), "trial and error" (performance tryouts), and "20 questions" (verbal instruction) are the most common and least effective ways to learn a job. To meet the training needs of an increasingly diverse workforce of individuals with different skills, abilities, and levels of experience, employers must provide more effective methods of OJT.

Benefits of Structured OJT

Because training is conducted at the job site, it has more relevance for the employee. The worker can practice new or enhanced skills immediately and become more confident and competent in the job more quickly. A structured OJT program builds teamwork and helps develop cohesiveness in the workgroup. Whether the employee receives training from a coworker or a supervisor, the fact that a person with whom the employee interacts daily is showing him or her "the ropes" will go a long way in establishing good interpersonal relations. Furthermore, ownership of the training ends where it belongs—with the individual department. Take a look now at Action Item 1.1.

➤ ACTION ITEM 1.1 ➤

Think about a situation where you were new to a job or had to learn a new task. What was the situation? How was the task presented to you? How did you feel? How successful were you in learning the new task? Do you wish the learning experience had been handled differently? If so, how? _____

_____

_____

_____

_____

_____

_____

_____

Making a Success of the Process

It has been estimated that 80 percent or more of all critical work skills is acquired on the job (Carnevale and Gainer 1989), but despite its importance most OJT is handled poorly. The process is generally sink or swim with very little support or guidance from the supervisor or fellow workers. The vignette "Sinking by Swimming" presents an example of just such a circumstance.

> ### VIGNETTE 1.1   SWIMMING BY SINKING
>
> *I experienced the sink-or-swim approach firsthand as a brand-new management trainee in a bank. I was assigned to the main office to learn the basics of retail banking and gain some experience dealing with customers. On my first day, I arrived early and introduced myself to the bank manager. After 30 minutes spent showing me where various files, forms, and manuals were located, he pointed out my desk, handed me a huge manual of New York State banking laws and procedures, and left me alone. For two weeks I sat there reading that gold manual. Strictly by trial and error I answered customer questions and opened new accounts. Every time I asked a colleague a question, I was told to "look it up." I felt stupid, inadequate, and frustrated. Finally, I couldn't take it any longer and requested reassignment to a branch where I would be trained. Unfortunately, the next assignment wasn't much better. The bank clearly had no plan in place to train any new employee, so I learned on my own by reading, asking questions of my fellow employees, and making a lot of mistakes along the way.*

Management support is critical to the success of any structured on-the-job training program. In addition to allocating time and the money for instructional resources and materials, rewards, and recognition, managers must recognize and promote the importance of training as a means of developing employees, improving the bottom line, and beating the competition.

For training to be successful, barriers such as time constraints, chaotic environments, and poor employee attitudes must be overcome. Training takes time but it's an investment that will result in increased worker competence and motivation. The employee gains self-esteem and heightened employment security; the organization benefits through greater productivity and profitability. Everybody wins.

⤝ ACTION ITEM 1.2 ⤝

When is training required? Take a moment and list some situations or circumstances in your company that call for directed instruction: _____

_____

_____

_____

_____

_____

Situations That Require Training

Training is obviously called for when an employee cannot perform a job because of a lack of knowledge, skills, and/or experience. This may include a new employee or one who has been with the organization but needs to be cross-trained or who has been assigned a new responsibility or moved to a different department.

Another situation requiring training involves new or changed job procedures. Corporate downsizing, reorganization, merger, process improvement, and reengineering often result in radically changed, streamlined, or newly developed procedures. These changes require experienced employees to learn new approaches to their work or, in many cases, to master totally new skills just to keep their jobs. When a merger occurs, for example, the acquiring organization will generally extend its existing policies and procedures as the standard operating procedure for the "new" organization. Employees from the acquired company may have to fill out new forms and learn new products and terminology. If one company is bought by another that's headquartered in a different country where the culture is quite different this is especially challenging.

Organizations engaged in process-improvement efforts may develop an entirely new way of doing a particular job that requires the people doing that job to learn the work all over again.

Rapidly changing technology is also affecting the need for training. Employees will need to be trained any time that new equipment or tools are introduced to the workplace. For example, if an organization converts its personal computers from one platform to another—let's say from Macintosh to IBM—employees will need to learn the new system. Introducing new software will also create a training need. Complete Action Item 1.2 now to identify some specific circumstances where training is needed.

In all these situations, a short session on dealing with individual change will help employees cope with the new learning experience and provide a context for them to grasp the need and purpose for the change. Workers will be much more receptive to the training if they understand clearly what has prompted the changes. They need to be reassured that the organization recognizes the difficulty they may have in making these adjustments and supports them by providing the training to do their jobs well and meet organizational expectations.

Yeah, But... Training Isn't *Always* the Answer

Training may not be the answer to a performance problem. Factors such as poor management or conditions beyond the employee's control may be at work. If the employee doesn't have the mental, physical, or emotional capability to do the job, training probably will be of little help. Differences in personal style may also prevent an employee from experiencing optimum success and satisfaction. There is a saying that "ducks don't climb trees," and we know from job-matching literature that all workers are not equally well suited for all positions (Barron, Black, and Lowenstein 1989). This fact grows more evident and critical as our population and workforce become more diverse.

As many of us have experienced, corporate America is fraught with "ducks" in jobs that really require "cats." An example: In my role as an internal consultant at a bank, a branch manager sent one of her tellers to me for career counseling. According to the manager, the teller was quite competent technically, performing her operational duties (such as balancing) accurately and efficiently. But she was a poor performer when it came to the *people* part of her job. She didn't interact well with coworkers and, although she wasn't rude to customers, she didn't exhibit the warm and caring behavior the bank expected of its frontline, customer-contact employees. We talked a long while and it was clear that we had a duck in a cat's job. In other words, the problem was that the teller didn't like working with people. Understanding that, we reassigned her to a back-office position in the mortgage department where she worked independently on her computer terminal, seldom interacting with coworkers and having no customer contact. She became a model employee! What this tells us is that training will not help the worker who has motivational or attitudinal problems that direct his or her performance.

It's important to make sure we address the cause, not the symptoms. Oftentimes the source of poor employee performance can be traced to the manager or to the organization itself. An employee who has had the proper training and has the knowledge, ability, and personal motivation to do the job but who is not performing satisfactorily may not be receiving the appropriate support or reinforcement from the supervisor. In some cases, the employee can't perform the job according to standards because the supervisor has not communicated those expectations clearly. In still other situations, the employee's tools and equipment may be causing the problem. See Action Item 1.3 below.

⚡ACTION ITEM 1.3 ⚡

Identify a situation in your work environment where an employee needs one-on-one training and then answer the following questions:

- ⚡ Who is the employee?
- ⚡ What is the employee's position?
- ⚡ What is the specific task for which he or she needs training?

_____
_____
_____

What barriers might hinder the employee's ability to perform this task?

_____
_____
_____

How might you overcome these barriers?

_____
_____
_____

Chapter 2
Training Adults

Chapter Objectives:
- Relate adult learning principles to OJT
- Identify ways to overcome resistance to learning
- Examine how the trainer holds the key to success

We learn all through our lives, in structured and freeform ways, and the nature and circumstances of each learning experience affect how and how much we learn. Consider some structured learning situations you've had and take the time to complete the Action Item below.

⇥ ACTION ITEM 2.1 ⇤

Recall a good and a bad learning experience. These can be taken from any time in your life (in elementary or high school, in college, in organizations, or at work). For each experience, briefly describe the highlights and list the factors that made the experience good or bad.

Description of Good Experience: _____
_____
_____
_____
_____

Factors That Made It Good: _____
_____
_____
_____
_____

Description of Bad Experience: _____
_____
_____
_____
_____

Factors That Made It Bad: _____
_____
_____
_____
_____

I've used this Action Item in many train-the-trainer programs and each time people come up with a list of positive factors that read like this:

➡ Teacher/trainer was patient.

➡ She encouraged students/learners.

➡ He used a variety of activities.

➡ She cared about both students/learners and subject.

➡ He was fair.

➡ Trainer let me know how I was doing.

➡ She knew the subject/job.

➡ Students/learners were involved.

➡ Class was fun.

➡ Teacher was well organized.

➡ Learning environment was nonthreatening.

➡ Teacher/trainer presented practical, realistic problems.

In contrast, examples of bad experiences created the following list:

➡ Teacher showed favoritism.

➡ Class was boring.

➡ Material was not relevant.

➡ Trainer was disorganized.

➡ He was threatening or intimidating.

➡ She didn't know subject/job.

➡ Teacher/trainer didn't respect students/learners.

Think about your feelings and reactions to both the good and bad experiences. How effective was each one? To what degree did the training or learning experience contribute to your success? When discussing questions in train-the-trainer programs, participants are quick to respond that the single most important contributor to the success or failure of the learning experience was the instructor. People often share how the good experiences had such a positive impact on their success in life and how the bad experiences created major obstacles to further education and training and, in some cases, prevented them from seeking or taking advantage of opportunities that could have led to career advancement.

Understanding Why People Learn

Although adult education theorists disagree on just how different adults are from children, most embrace the *andragogical theory* of adult learning (in contrast to the *pedagogical* or child-centered model). During the 1960s, European adult educators coined the term *andragogy* to label a growing body of knowledge and technology centered on adult learning. The concept was introduced and advanced in the United States by Malcolm Knowles. The following five assumptions underlie the andragogical model of learning, which Knowles now calls a model of *human* learning, and they can guide trainers in crafting successful instructional programs:

Why Adults Learn
✔ Adults are self-directed learners.
✔ Adults build on prior experience.
✔ Adults respond to a need to perform more effectively.
✔ Adults want real-world applications for learning.
✔ Adults are motivated by internal factors.

The learner is self-directing. Adult learners want to take responsibility for their own lives, including planning, implementing, and evaluating their learning activities. From the beginning the trainer needs to establish the training process as a collaborative effort, and throughout the process both parties should be partners engaged in ongoing two-way communication.

Adults build on prior experience. According to Knowles, each of us brings to a learning situation a wealth of experience that provides a base for new learning and serves as a resource to share with others. Good or bad, the prior experience will affect the way an employee approaches a new task, and the new information will have to be assimilated. The savvy trainer determines what the trainee already knows and builds on that experience instead of assuming he or she knows nothing and must be "taught" like a small child.

Adults are ready to learn when they see a need to know or do something in order to perform more effectively. The days of abstract theories and concepts are over for most adults. They want the learning experience to be practical and realistic. The effective trainer helps the trainee understand how mastering a particular skill or task will boost job success, that is, how the employee can do the job quicker, easier, or more efficiently. This is particularly important in a retraining situation where the employee may resist the change.

Adults want real-world application now. They want the skills and knowledge to help them complete tasks or solve problems they are currently confronting. People are motivated to learn when the topic is relevant to their lives and they want to apply the learning as quickly as possible. Therefore, effective trainers deliver just-in-time training and they emphasize how the new skill will make work easier.

Adults are motivated to learn by internal factors. Internal motivators such as self-esteem, recognition, natural curiosity, innate love of learning, better quality of life, enhanced self-confidence, or the opportunity to self-actualize drive the adult learner (Knowles 1990). Just as people work for different reasons, they want to learn for different reasons. The effective trainer identifies the trainee's WIIFM (What's In It For Me?) and clearly links it to the training.

Think about an adult learning experience you have had. Were you treated as an adult? Did the teacher or trainer acknowledge the experience and knowledge you brought to the learning situation? Or were you assumed to be a blank slate who needed to be told and controlled?

Most trainers approach their task the way they were taught. In many cases, the only learning experience they've had is the traditional teacher-student relationship they experienced as children in school. Almost all of us have come through the pedagogical model of learning that has dominated education and training for centuries. We take that as our model when we train others. In brief, the child-centered model makes the following assumptions:

➡ The teacher is responsible for the learning process, including what and how learners learn. The learner takes a passive role.

➡ The learner has little experience, and the teacher is the expert, the guru. He or she must impart a body of knowledge in what amounts to an "information dump" through the traditional means of lecture, textbooks, manuals, or videos in which other experts share what they know.

➡ People are motivated to learn because they have to in order to pass a test, advance to the next level, or earn certification.

➡ Learning is information centered. The teacher covers the material so that the learner gets the prescribed information in some sort of logical order.

➡ Motivation to learn is largely external. Pressure from authority figures and fear of negative consequences drive the learner. The teacher, in essence, controls the learning through rewards and discipline.

If you compare these assumptions with those of the andragogical model you can see the striking contrasts and how using the pedagogical theory will not promote successful OJT.

Understanding How People Learn

Before you train or designate someone else to do so, there are several other principles to keep in mind about how adults learn.

No single way of presenting information suits everyone. One person may learn best by listening. Another may be visual and prefer to read instructions or look at a diagram. Someone else will need a demonstration. If you have any doubts about this, try Action Item 2.2 below.

⤝ ACTION ITEM 2.2 ⤞

Ask someone to learn fancy napkin folding.

- ⤝ Give the trainee a cloth or paper napkin.
- ⤝ Show the trainee a napkin folded artistically as you would find in a fine restaurant. Use either a picture or an actual folded napkin.
- ⤝ Instruct the trainee to fold his or her napkin to duplicate the sample.
- ⤝ After a few moments of watching the trainee struggle, ask how he or she feels. More than likely, the trainee will say something like, "I'm frustrated (stupid, incompetent, awkward)."
- ⤝ Now tell the trainee how to accomplish the fold and ask for another attempt.
- ⤝ If that isn't adequate, offer written instructions.
- ⤝ If the trainee still is not successful, provide a diagram.
- ⤝ If that isn't helpful, demonstrate how to fold the napkin.

This activity is particularly effective with a group. You'll find that some people are able to fold the napkin correctly once they read the written instructions; others will need the additional diagram; still others can only follow a demonstration. This is an excellent way to discover the different ways in which people learn and it helps point out that an instructor needs to adjust the training style to accommodate the learning style.

David Kolb's *Learning Style Inventory* (1981) is an excellent way to identify one's own learning style and develop an appreciation for others' styles. Kolb identifies the following four learning methods:

Who Are You Training?

✔ The Concrete Experiencer
✔ The Reflective Observer
✔ The Abstract Conceptualizer
✔ The Active Experimenter

Concrete Experience. People who favor this mode learn through feeling rather than thinking. They like to be involved with people, and they prefer less structure in the learning environment. They approach learning with an open mind.

Reflective Observation. This mode focuses on learning by watching and observing. These learners try to understand the meaning of ideas and situations by observing them and objectively describing what they see.

Abstract Conceptualization. Those who learn by this method prefer thinking over feeling. They take a scientific, systematic approach to learning.

Active Experimentation. With the emphasis on practical application, learners who prefer this mode are action-oriented and want to get things done. They take risks.

To identify your learning style, see Action Item below. Read the situation and follow the directions.

✎ ACTION ITEM 2.3 ✎

Imagine that you have just bought a new car with a standard transmission. Although you've been driving for many years, you have no idea how to drive a stickshift. Rank-order the following approaches according to their importance to you in learning this new skill (1 = most importance; 4 = least important):

_____ I want to be given the keys and allowed to try it myself in a parking lot.

_____ I want an instructor who is patient and coaches me as I try it myself.

_____ I want to read the manual to get an idea of how the clutch and the gearshift work. Then I want a step-by-step explanation of how to do it.

_____ I want to sit in the passenger seat and observe my instructor. When I try it myself, I want a flat surface with no one else around, and I want ample opportunity to practice before going out into traffic.

If you choose the first approach as the most important to you, you are most likely an Active Experimenter. You learn by doing. You're action oriented, enjoy being challenged, and tend to make decisions quickly. Learning on your own is quite comfortable and the instructor is insignificant.

If you ranked the second item as 1, you may be a Concrete Experiencer. You have a short attention span and dislike details. You learn from feeling. Because you're a caring, sensitive person, your instructor needs to create a comfortable learning environment.

If item 3 was your first choice, Abstract Conceptualization is probably your preferred learning mode. You learn by thinking, approach tasks systematically, and want to know as much as you can about the situation before you begin. Your instructor must provide details and a thorough explanation.

Finally, if you rated the last approach as most important, your preferred learning mode may be Reflective Observation. You learn by watching and listening. By nature a perfectionist, you're cautious and want to make sure you do it right. Your instructor needs to provide adequate opportunities to try out the task or skill before you actually apply it on the job.

Remember that no one learning mode is better than another. Everyone learns differently, and the effective trainer recognizes these style variations and adapts his or her style to suit them.

Perceptual Modalities: How Information Gets Inside

Trainers planning successful strategies must understand that a learner may prefer one or another of the following ways to take in and process information (James and Galbraith 1985):

Perceptual Modality	Training Aids and Activities
Visual	Videos, slides, graphs, photos, demonstrations, exhibits
Print	Texts, paper-and-pencil exercises
Aural	Lectures, audiotapes
Interactive	Group discussions, question-and-answer sessions
Tactile	Hands-on activities, model-building
Kinesthetic	Role plays, physical games and activities

How People Take In and Process Information
✔ Visually
✔ Via print
✔ Aurally
✔ Interactively
✔ Tactilely
✔ Kinesthetically

Every good training design, including one for OJT, will incorporate all six modalities to ensure that each trainee's needs are being addressed. For example, let's look at a design for training someone to use a personal computer. The trainer makes sure the instruction includes a computer screen or, at the very least, pictures of the screen to illustrate what happens there when a particular key is struck. The instructor demonstrates how to perform certain functions on the computer (*visual*). The training plan includes print materials such as a manual and short application-oriented quizzes (*print*). For review and rein-forcement, the instructor may prepare an audiotape (*aural*). During daily training sessions, there are many opportunities for the trainee to ask and answer questions (*interactive*) and to have hands-on practice (*tactile*). Finally, the instructor creates simulation activities in which the trainee produces actual work-related documents such as spreadsheets, reports, and graphs (*kinesthetic*).

Telling Is *Not* Training

Telling is not teaching or training. How many times have you said to yourself, "I've told him and told him how to do it, but he still gets it wrong?" Your describing a process doesn't ensure that the listener understands it or has developed the skill to do it.

This is a vital distinction: People generally learn by doing, not by being told how to do something. For example, you'll learn more quickly how to reach a new location if you're the driver instead of the passenger. The more times a person can try out new skills or apply new knowledge, the more likely he or she is to learn the skills and details.

That Issue of Age

One issue that comes up frequently in train-the-trainer and coaching courses involves the impact of age on the learning process. Managers, supervisors, and trainers often say that "older" workers are slower and more difficult to train. (I always ask for a definition of "older" and, much to my dismay, the most common response is "over 40.")

Researchers are divided on the relationship of age and ability to learn, depending on how each interprets "learning." In general, research suggests that adults continue to learn throughout the years but that we may take longer to grasp new things. Although younger people seem to be more efficient when it comes to memorizing information, as we grow older we are better able to evaluate and apply information (Cross 1980). Research shows that "change in adulthood is a procession of critical periods during the fifty-plus years following childhood and youth. These periods consist of marked changes and experiences during which some of the most meaningful learning may occur" (McClusky 1970). We must recognize, of course, that physical changes play a part in the learning process. As we age, we may experience hearing loss, lower energy levels, and slower reaction times. But these changes are not proof that older people are slower or have greater difficulty learning.

By observing adult learning principles and accommodating the essential differences among individuals, an instructor can be successful in training any adult.

Process Is the Key to Successful Training

The traditional or pedagogical model of instruction is concerned with content. Trainers following this model focus on covering material by the most efficient means possible. In contrast, the andragogical model focuses on *process* and trainers who are process-oriented attend to the following:

1. Creating a positive learning climate

2. Involving learners in planning for their learning

3. Involving learners in identifying their own needs

4. Involving learners in setting their learning objectives

5. Involving learners in designing their learning plans

6. Helping learners carry out their learning plans

7. Involving learners in evaluating their own learning outcomes.

All training, even task-oriented OJT, lends itself to a process designed around these seven principles.

Cooperative Learning

By nature, we are social beings. Effective trainers capitalize on this elemental characteristic by using cooperative learning techniques when more than one person is being trained for the same skill or task. The basic principle of cooperative learning is that people "work together to maximize their own and each others' learning" (Johnson, Johnson, and Smith 1991). This approach is based on two assumptions: (a) learning is an active endeavor and (b) different people learn in different ways (Meyers and Jones 1993).

As an example, let's assume you have two people who are learning a new presentation graphics computer program. To promote cooperative learning and spur synergy between them, present some content-related questions to review material already covered or arouse curiosity and interest in what you are about to introduce. You might ask:

➡ What is the recommended number of lines per page for a transparency or slide?

➡ How many ways can you display a presentation?

➡ Where is the spelling tool located?

Instruct both trainees to write answers to each question. Then ask them to work together to create new answers and to share these cooperatively improved ones with you. You'll correct, clarify, or expand on their responses and they'll learn, additionally, how joint efforts enhance success.

When training adults, the most important thing to remember is just that—they're adults!

Chapter 3
Selecting the Trainer

Chapter Objectives:
- Explore the importance of selecting the right person as a trainer
- Identify the personal qualities, characteristics, and competencies for on-the-job trainers
- Assess your perception of potential candidates' qualifications
- Develop a process for delegating training responsibilities to qualified employees

As a result of downsizing and outsourcing, on-staff trainers are scarce. Few organizations are fortunate enough to have a full-time training department equipped to meet all the organization's needs, especially the growing demand for one-on-one OJT. As a consequence, companies must rely on first-line supervisors or designated peer trainers to prepare employees to do their jobs. Selecting the right person to do the training is critical.

At first blush, the task seems simple enough: We'll just choose the person who's been around the longest, who does the job the best, or who has the extra time. Problem solved. *Wrong!* Selecting the right trainer is integral to the success of the training process and should never be done thoughtlessly. Not everyone is cut out to be a trainer, and smart selection requires careful assessment of well-considered criteria.

Advantages of Peer Trainers

Peer trainers have the distinct advantage of credibility because they've "been there, done that." Using experienced employees to train their coworkers gives more people an opportunity to be involved and to share with others what they know and what they've done. Peer trainers are often more effective than supervisors because trainees may be easily intimidated by receiving training from the person to whom they ultimately report. An added bonus to the peer-training approach is job enhancement for the person designated as a trainer.

Drawbacks to the Buddy System

One potential negative to peer teaching is that the experienced person may know the job so well that he or she skips important basic information. Or the trainer regularly may take shortcuts that are clear violations of standard company or department procedure but that are not challenged because the trainer has tenure or is highly competent overall. If this trainer passes along these shortcuts, the trainee picks up bad habits.

Another drawback is job overload. Unless given a reprieve from some of his or her typical responsibilities, the trainer is often too busy to answer the trainee's questions. Holes or gaps result and there is a loss of continuity in the training. The trainee is forced into a trial-and-error learning mode and will likely experience frustration and a sense of failure.

What to Look for in a Trainer Candidate:

✔ Job competence
✔ Good communication skills
✔ Professionalism
✔ Good interpersonal skills
✔ Well-developed time management and organizing skills
✔ Patience and flexibility
✔ Innovation and initiative
✔ Team spirit

Choosing the Right Person for the Training Task

Although good trainers can be developed, certain competencies should be prerequisites to their training skill development.

Let's begin by discovering what you think qualifies a person to train others. Complete Action Item 3.1 below; then come back for a discussion of needed characteristics.

⚡ ACTION ITEM 3.1 ⚡

Identify someone on your staff that you think would be a good trainer. List that person's qualities, skills, and characteristics to support your choice.

Trainer Candidate's Name: _____

Job/Task to Be Taught: _____

Trainer Candidate's Specific Qualifications:_____

_____

_____

_____

_____

_____

The Right Stuff

In making your selection of a potential trainer, look for the following qualifications.

Job Competence

The most obvious qualification is the ability to do the job well. Trainers need the appropriate technical knowledge and experience in doing the job. But remember that just being good at one's job doesn't guarantee being able to teach someone else to do the same work.

Good Communication Skills

When I ask line managers and supervisors to list requisite skills, qualities, or characteristics of an effective trainer, the ability to communicate well is cited every time as the most crucial skill contributing to a trainer's success, after job competence. The trainer must be lucid in describing tasks and procedures and must be an active listener as well. He or she must be sensitive to everyone's body language. Encouraging questions establishes an open flow of communication and creates a nonthreatening environment where the trainee can take risks and make mistakes without fear of being judged stupid or incompetent.

Professionalism

Because the trainer is a role model, he or she should be mature, confident, and enthusiastic. This should be someone eager to expand current job responsibilities who sees this additional assignment as an opportunity to grow professionally rather than an intrusion in the daily routine. The trainer's professional manner should be marked by a high energy level, appropriate dress, good work habits, and a strong desire to contribute to the organization's success. Along these lines, it is equally vital that the trainer believes in his or her own competence and demonstrates that confidence without arrogance.

Interpersonal Skills

In choosing part-time trainers, look for people who demonstrate good interpersonal skills in a variety of situations with coworkers and people outside of the organization. They should be friendly, congenial, and able to manage conflict without "losing their cool." Particularly with newly hired workers, the trainer's sociability can be helpful in assimilating trainees into the work environment. The trainer must also be empathetic and nurturing, supporting and encouraging the trainee, and giving positive reinforcement and feedback throughout the training process.

Good Organizational and Time Management Skills

Good organizational skills are significant contributors to training success. Demonstrated ability to organize the workarea and workflow and to manage time competently are trainer prerequisites. How the trainer organizes and manages both self and work will carry over to how he or she develops and implements a training plan. Organizational skills also include the capacity to put one's thoughts in order before trying to communicate them.

Patience and Flexibility

Although well planned and structured for focus, training is not a rigid process. If a trainee doesn't pick up a task or grasp the information right away, the trainer will need to adjust the schedule and try different ways of getting the point across, of helping the trainee understand and succeed.

Innovation and Initiative

As a role model, a good trainer demonstrates qualities such as creativity, innovation, and initiative. By example, these traits are built into the job and passed on to the trainee.

Team Spirit

The trainer needs a sense of commitment to training the employee and should take pride in the trainee's success, sharing a sense of teamwork. This type of peer training builds a strong and healthy working relationship that continues beyond the training experience. It helps trainer and trainee develop their own network and strengthens the team concept.

Making Assumptions About Trainer Candidates

Now you know that choosing a trainer is not as easy as you first thought. Let's get more specific. To identify a likely candidate, you have to make assumptions about his or her personal and professional suitability.

One way to determine if an employee has "trainer potential" is to ask yourself the following questions:

Does this employee…
1. Communicate well by organizing thoughts, choosing appropriate words, and speaking clearly and distinctly?
2. Practice good time management by completing assignments on time, organizing duties logically, breaking projects down into tasks and subtasks, and so on?
3. Get along well with others at all levels?
4. Exemplify in both manner and appearance those qualities you want others to emulate?
5. Know the job, perform well above average, and meet or exceed job standards and expectations?

Figure 3.1. Selection Criteria Matrix

Candidate	Job Knowledge	Communication Skills	Professionalism	Interpersonal Skills

6. Exercise patience and self-control even when things are not going well?
7. Look for ways to improve the job and seek opportunities to assume more responsibility?
8. Welcome new ideas and regard change positively?
9. Display nonarrogant confidence in his or her own ability to do the job?
10. Support the philosophy and goals of the organization and the department?
11. Practice as well as believe in teamwork?
12. Demonstrate a willingness to help others even if "it's not my job?"

If you can answer *yes* to at least nine of these 12 questions, you have identified a person who should do well as a trainer. If you scored the candidate lower than nine, take a look at the questions to which you answered *no* and identify ways to help this person improve.

Testing Your Assumptions in an Interview

The next and most critical step in selecting a trainer is to test your assumptions about a person's suitability by establishing specific, behavior-based selection criteria and interviewing all the candidates.

Before the interviews, create a *Selection Criteria Matrix* (Figure 3.1) to use in evaluating each of the candidates. On this matrix put cells for each of the qualities and capabilities you consider important. You should devise a rating system and assign a point value to evaluate each candidate's strength in each criterion. For example, 4 points may indicate a superior rating; 3 points, above average; 2 points, good; and 1 point, acceptable. During or immediately following the interview, score each candidate on the matrix.

What follow are some interview questions to help you determine to what degree the candidate practices the skills or possesses the qualities on the matrix:

➡ What experience have you had in training others?

Organizational and Time Management Skills	Flexibility	Creativity	Innovation	Initiative	Team Spirit

➡ What do you like best about training someone on the job?

➡ What do you dislike about it?

➡ What are your skills or qualities that will make you a successful trainer?

➡ How have you handled (or will you handle) your regular workload while taking on the additional training responsibility?

➡ What do you see (or anticipate) as the biggest problem or barrier in training someone?

➡ How have you handled this problem or barrier in the past (or how will you handle this barrier)?

➡ How did you learn to do your job?

➡ What did you like or dislike about the way you learned?

These questions will not only provide you with insight into the candidate's training skills but also his or her general attitude in assuming additional responsibilities.

Delegating the Assignment to the Chosen Trainer

When you've chosen a trainer, your next step is to delegate the task to that person. Remember that effective delegating requires good communication and a high degree of trust between the parties involved.

Task Delegating Isn't...and Is...

First, keep in mind that delegating is *not* task assignment. It isn't simply handing off to an individual some work within the duties and responsibilities of his or her position. Delegating involves the manager giving someone the responsibility and authority to do something that is normally part of the *manager's* job. Clearly, training employees to do their jobs is a manager's responsibility, directly or indirectly.

Responsibility + Authority + Accountability

Second, delegation is not "dumping." Take special care to ensure that the employee doesn't think you're trying to unload an unpleasant assignment. If delegating is not done properly, employees feel put upon and resent what they perceive as doing the boss's work.

The third point is that delegating is not abdicating. The manager still has the ultimate accountability for the assignment. In this case, you as the manager may be one-step-removed from the actual training but through your choice of trainer you are accountable if the employee does not acquire the skills and knowledge to do the job.

Delegating involves three important factors: Responsibility, authority, and accountability. When you delegate, you share responsibility and authority with others and you hold them accountable for their performance. *Responsibility* refers to the assignment itself and its intended results. Sharing responsibility means setting and communicating clear expectations and performance criteria, including specific time frames and a standardized approach to the training process. *Authority* refers to the appropriate power given to the individual, including the right to act and make decisions. In relation to this factor, it's very important to communicate boundaries such as budgetary considerations. *Accountability* refers to the delegatee's need to answer for his or her actions and decisions and to his or her ownership of the rewards or penalties that accompany those actions or decisions.

The Delegating Process

Before you approach the employee with this new assignment, take the time to plan how you're going to present the assignment, including your requirements, parameters, authority level, checkpoints, and expectations. It's a good idea to write down these items and give a copy to your delegatee to minimize miscommunication.

Think about how the employee will react. You may think you're doing a great thing by delegating the training assignment to this person, but will he or she see it the same way? It's easy to assume the employee knows and understands your motivation, but quite often, the employee perceives that advantage is being taken instead. To prevent this, identify the benefits to the employee and be sure to communicate these benefits clearly.

Think about the potential trainer's personality as well as his or her skills. This is an important consideration when presenting the assignment to the chosen person. Some people may want and need a great deal of detail and explanation; others respond better to a simple statement of expectations and guidelines, then want to be left alone to "go to it."

When you sit down with your employee to delegate the training assignment, follow the seven steps described below. For a real-world view of such a situation, read how a manager delegated a training assignment to Juan (page 26).

How to Delegate the Training Task
✔ Give an overview of the assignment
✔ Explain the training assignment in detail
✔ Alleviate the new trainer's concerns
✔ Solicit input from the chosen trainer
✔ Ask for commitment
✔ Arrange for follow-up
✔ Define the resulting reward and recognition for successful task completion

Step One: Give an Overview of the Assignment

Start by explaining to the trainer the importance of the assignment and why you have chosen him or her for these training responsibilities. Refer to the list of assumptions you prepared earlier and to the criteria selection matrix to help you identify and communicate the specific qualities and skills that ideally qualify this person. Be sure to stress the ways this new assignment will benefit the employee.

Step Two: Explain the Assignment

Describe the new responsibility in detail, outlining tasks and subtasks, defining necessary parameters, and setting performance standards for the trainer and the trainee(s). Make certain the person understands the level or degree of authority that is being conferred. Let the employee know to whom he can turn for help and other resources. In addition, be sure to notify those affected by the trainer's increased authority.

Step Three: Alleviate Concerns

At this point, it's a good idea to anticipate and alleviate any concerns the employee has about this new responsibility. Assure the designated trainer that you will make sure she attends a train-the-trainer program and receives the appropriate tools and resources to do the job. Also address the time demands created by this new assignment and any necessary reassigning of the employee's current responsibilities to other workers until the training assignment is complete. An employee who already feels overwhelmed may worry about completing the work already expected. It's your responsibility to help establish priorities and relieve some of the pressure by getting someone to share some of the employee's routine tasks for the duration of the training assignment.

Step Four: Solicit Input

Ask the employee to share questions, reactions, concerns, or suggestions. Ask what problems or barriers he or she anticipates that you have not considered. You might also ask the employee to suggest how the workload can be redistributed during this interim period. Listen to the employee's comments and respond empathetically.

Step Five: Ask for Commitment

This step helps to get the employee to buy into the assignment and will help you determine if the employee does indeed understand your expectations. Be encouraging and express your confidence in the employee's ability to succeed in this new assignment.

Step Six: Arrange for Follow-up

Establish checkpoints, deadlines, and ways to monitor progress. You will want to meet periodically with the trainer to monitor his or her growth and progress as a trainer and to receive feedback about the progress of the employee(s) being trained. Remember that delegating means letting go. When training begins, keep in contact with the trainer and observe the checkpoints the two of you established. But don't hover or micromanage.

Step Seven: Define the Rewards

At this point in delegating, describe the reward and recognition the employee can expect when the training has been successfully completed. We will discuss specific measurements and rewards in later chapters.

Now think about a training responsibility you need to delegate. In Action Item 3.2, outline your approach using the seven-step model described above.

⚡ACTION ITEM 3.2 ⚡

Step One: Give an overview of assignment _____
_____
_____

Step Two: Explain the details _____
_____
_____

Step Three: Alleviate concerns _____
_____
_____

Step Four: Solicit input _____
_____
_____

Step Five: Ask for commitment _____
_____
_____

Step Six: Arrange for follow-up_____
_____
_____

Step Seven: Define the reward_____
_____
_____

Reaping the Benefits

Carefully selecting trainers and structuring the training process will ensure success for the employees, the manager, and the organization. The new trainer grows professionally by developing interpersonal, communication, organizational, and problem-solving skills. On-the-job training assignments also yield personal satisfaction and a sense of achievement. They open doors to greater involvement in decision making which in turn leads to increased commitment and higher morale. In general, these opportunities enhance the employee's value to the organization.

Employees being trained will benefit from the high level of quality training being delivered by a peer who is not only capable but also committed to making sure each trainee receives the skills and knowledge to do his or her job. Managers will experience less stress because they have well-trained employees performing their tasks efficiently and effectively. Managers will also be freer to spend their time dealing with higher-level problem solving and visioning rather than worrying about training problems. Organizations, of course, will benefit from having skilled, high-performance workers delivering quality products and services, and that leads directly to increased profitability.

VIGNETTE 3.1 JUAN GETS THE NOD: DELEGATING THE ASSIGNMENT TO A NEW TRAINER

Step One. *Juan, I want to talk to you about possibly taking on a new assignment—one that's not only vital to the successful operation of our department, but one I believe will be of benefit to you personally. You've been doing an excellent job with the new computer system. I'm really impressed with how quickly you've adapted to the new platform. I've noticed you not only understand the concepts and applications, but you're patient and clear in your explanations when someone asks you a question about a particular application. You seem to have a natural flair for explaining procedures to others. For that reason, I'm asking you to take on the new responsibility of department trainer. If we're going to maintain our high performance standards, we have to get everyone in the department up to speed as quickly as possible, and I believe you're the best person to make that happen. [Pause to let Juan respond.]*

Step Two. *It will be your responsibility to set up a training schedule for each person in the department. We're aiming for consistency so I'll also expect you to develop a training plan to ensure that each person is trained the same way. We're on a tight timeline. We need this plan in two months. It will be up to you to determine how you will evaluate each person's competency. I'll make sure that each person in the department understands your new responsibility and that you are completely in charge of the training project. This is your baby, and I'm here to support you along the way.*

Step Three. *I can imagine you might have some concerns about this project, especially since you have had no formal experience in training techniques. If you agree to take on this assignment, I'll arrange for you to attend a three-day train-the-trainer program being offered next week. In addition to that resource, our internal training department will be more than happy to offer whatever support and materials you need. I suggest you meet with them within the next two days to get some additional guidance and direction. I also suggest that you contact our computer vendor and support service to see what training materials they have and what help they can offer. But, Juan, the bottom line is that you will be doing the individual training. This assignment is a top priority. I recognize that you already have a full workload so I'll take on the task of dividing your existing assignments and responsibilities among your coworkers until this training is complete.*

Step Four. *I know I've hit you with a lot all at once, Juan, but what is your initial reaction? The look on your face suggests that you'd like to take on this assignment. Am I right?…What are some potential problems or barriers I might have overlooked?…What can I do to help?…What ideas do you have for redistributing the workload so that it's fair and equitable?*

Step Five. *Juan, do I have your commitment?…I know you'll do a great job of training and leading this entire project. As I said earlier, I believe you have natural talent and your coworkers really respect you. Although there are no guarantees, this experience will certainly broaden your background and help prepare you for a number of different positions within the company. You'll be developing a valuable skill you can take anywhere.*

Step Six. *It's important that we meet regularly to monitor progress. Let's plan on getting together the day after you've finished your train-the-trainer program. And at that time we can set up weekly meetings to discuss the progress of each person you're teaching and also discuss your progress in developing your training skills.*

Step Seven. *If we're successful in getting everyone up to speed within our time frame, I'll make sure you get the proper credit and reward, Juan. I really appreciate your taking on this assignment.*

Chapter 4
Developing a Training Plan

Chapter Objectives:
- Break down the job into separate tasks and subtasks
- Determine observable and measurable standards of performance
- Write performance objectives that measure training outcomes or results
- Write detailed training plans that incorporate an instructional timetable
- Devise training methods that prompt the trainee to discover information cognitively, behaviorally, and affectively
- Identify the role of job aids in OJT
- Create teaching aids to increase learning effectiveness

Remember that OJT focuses on individual tasks, not the entire job. It is concerned specifically with behaviors, thoughts, and decisions, and with their resulting performance outcomes. Outcomes focus on quality, quantity, timeliness, cost, and so forth. The first step in designing a training plan is doing a task analysis to identify all of the steps or subtasks of a particular job.

A task or job analysis can be as simple or as complex as you want it to be. A starting point for a comprehensive, complex approach might involve interviewing people who've already done the job, their supervisors, and customers one-on-one or in focus groups. It might involve observing people at work, reviewing performance appraisals, and reading or talking to experts in the field.

Analyzing Job Tasks and Setting Standards

Before we can develop a plan of instruction for OJT, we must break the job down into tasks and then into steps or subtasks. Breaking large tasks into smaller ones prevents the trainee from feeling overwhelmed and makes it easier for the trainee to master by increasing understanding and proficiency one step at a time. Subtasks lend themselves to smaller incremental goals, giving the trainee an opportunity to experience frequent and multiple successes along the way. This intrinsic reward system motivates the trainee and that results in less frustration and greater satisfaction with the learning experience.

Every job has a number of actions that must be completed to get the job done. Take a look at the sidebar that details some of the tasks involved in a secretary's job (page 30). The core tasks break down into levels of subtasks and then into steps, becoming more precise at each more elemental level (see the step breakdown for answering the telephone).

Task Breakdown: The Secretary's Job

✔ Handle telephone communications

   — answer the telephone

     1. Pick up the receiver.

     2. Greet the caller, identify yourself and/or the department, and ask how you may be of help.

     3. Respond to the caller's request.

     4. Complete the telephone interaction by asking if there is anything else you can do.

     5. Replace the receiver.

   — place outgoing calls for boss(es)

   — screen calls

✔ Manage office procedures

   — maintain appointment calendar

   — make travel arrangements

   — set up meetings

   — prepare expense reports

   — maintain filing system

   — process daily mail

✔ Handle correspondence

   — transcribe dictation

   — prepare letters and memos as directed

   — draft letters and memos as directed

We should also note that part of effective training is defining performance standards and these are defined at the most specific step level of each task. Without identifying task details, setting standards is impossible.

In the case of answering the telephone, performance standards might include answering within a prescribed number of rings (preferably no more than three); greeting the caller by saying, "Good morning (afternoon)" in a pleasant voice; stating one's first and last names; and asking, "How may I help you?" These are just the standards for steps one and two. Without these standards identified and spelled out for the employee during training, the secretary is at liberty to allow the telephone to ring multiple times and answer it in any way he or she chooses.

Standards of performance must be observable (you can see the secretary picking up the receiver and greeting the caller), measurable (the secretary picks up the telephone in three rings), and attainable (the secretary has the ability to answer the telephone according to the prescribed company procedure).

An easy and effective aid to identifying tasks, breaking them down into subtasks and steps, and delineating the appropriate performance standards is the Job/Task Analysis Chart (Figure 4.1).

Standards of Performance Must Be:

✔ Observable
✔ Measurable
✔ Attainable

Figure 4.1 Job/Task Analysis Chart

Step	What	How	Why

Notice that each step on the chart identifies three key components: What, how, and why. *What* describes the activity; *how* defines the way in which the step should be completed (the performance standards) and includes tools and equipment; the *why* explains the reason for doing the step.

To illustrate this further, let's take a look at a common multistep task: Washing a car. The overall objective and standard of performance is to wash the car, inside and out, within three hours. Figure 4.2 is a completed job/task analysis chart for the first few steps.

Figure 4.2 Sample Job/Task Analysis: Washing a Car

Step	What	How	Why
1.	Assemble materials	Bucket, sponges, hose, cleaning agent, glass cleaner, chamois, paper towels, chrome cleaner, vacuum	To make process more efficient and prevent tracking water in the house if you forget something
2.	Position car	Move car close to water supply and out of direct sun	To prevent damage to paint resulting from contrasting temperatures
3.	Apply water to car	Hose entire car surface	To eliminate surface dirt and prevent scratching the paint

To practice breaking large jobs into their more manageable subtasks, go to Action Item 4.1.

⤙ Action Item 4.1 ⤚

Choose a task you perform in your job and list the major steps a person would have to follow to perform that task successfully. List those steps in the *What* column of the job/task analysis chart below. Then fill in the *How* and *Why* columns for each step. Be sure to identify the standard of performance for each step.

Step	What	How	Why

Setting Objectives

As we prepare our training plan, the performance standards now become the basis for a training objective, which in turn serves as a means to measure results. For training purposes, performance standards are written as objectives (performance outcomes) and include the following components:

➡ An action or behavior that refers to the content or object. It must be an action verb, such as *write, assemble,* or *build.*

➡ A standard or criterion by which performance will be measured. Such criteria include speed (within 15 minutes), accuracy (100 percent), quantity (minimum of...), quality (no errors), and time or frequency (daily, weekly).

➡ A condition or situation that describes where the task is to be performed; what limitations, conditions, or constraints may affect performance; or what materials or equipment will be used.

The following model is helpful in writing an objective with standards: *As a result of this training, the trainee will be able to...(action), (criteria or standards of performance), (con-*

dition). *Applying the model to our common task of washing a car, the objective might be:* The person will be able to wash the car inside and outside *(action)* within three hours *(criteria)* using available materials and equipment and according to standard procedures as outlined in the procedures manual *(condition)*. Now try this yourself in Action Item 4.2.

➤ ACTION ITEM 4.2 ➤

For the tasks you identified in Action Item 4.1, write an objective for a new employee.

_____

_____

_____

_____

_____

The Instructional Plan, From General to Specific

The instructional plan links content and events. In other words, the plan identifies what the trainer is going to communicate (content points) and how the trainer is going to communicate the information or develop a particular skill (methods).

Sketch It In—The General Content and Timeline

After you've determined the training objectives, create an outline with a timeline. The outline or training design matrix simply lists the topics to be covered and the amount of time you'll devote to each. It may also include activities and materials, such as manuals or other training aids. A copy of the outline and timetable should be given to trainees so that they know exactly what to expect. It allows them to do some self-monitoring and lets

Figure 4.3 Training Design Matrix and Timeline

Duration	Content/Teaching Points	Methods/Activity	Materials/Aids

them know that they must take responsibility for their learning. Figure 4.3 is a Training Design Matrix.

Spell It Out—The Detailed Instructional Plan

Using the rough outline in the design matrix, you now build a more detailed instructional plan (see the example in Figure 4.4). The instructional plan should also list materials needed (equipment, supplies) and resources (people, manuals). Each section of the plan should include the objective(s) stated precisely and in observable and measurable terms so the trainee knows what will be learned each day. This plan goes into great detail not only about what content will be covered but also how the trainer is going to do it and with what resources.

The training plan should build incrementally and be delivered at a pace appropriate to the learner's experience and ability. It should allow for individual differences and be de-

Figure 4.4 Sample Instructional Plan for Training a Bank Teller

Objectives:
— Identify the security procedures necessary prior to the branch opening.
— Set up and organize the teller window with the necessary supplies.
— Use the proper procedures in ordering cash from the vault for the teller drawer.

Training Aids:
— Teller Manual pp. 1-22

Outline:

Time	Major Points	Aid	Teaching Notes
9:00	I. Opening Procedures		
	A. Security		
	1. Vault versus cash cart		Show cash cart
	2. Vault under dual control		
9:15	B. Physical set-up of teller window		Take trainee(s)
	1. Supplies		behind teller line
	2.Organization		and show where
	3. Bait money		bait is kept; how
	4. Alarm button		to activate alarm
9:30	C. Proving the cash drawer	pp. 4-6	
	1. Reasons		
	2. Procedures		
	D. Ordering cash		
	1. Cash memo	TR1	
	2. Ordering procedures		
	3. Branch and individual cash limits	FC	Explain why
	4. Mutilated and Canadian funds		
10:00	E. Terminal activity		
	1. Sign on procedures		Explain and
	2. Identification codes		demonstrate
	F. Application		Have trainee(s)
	1. Cash drawer worksheet	HO1	practice signing
	2. Keyboard exercise		on

livered just-in-time so that the trainee can soon begin applying and practicing what's been learned. And it should include a means of testing both what's been learned and how capably it's applied or performed in real-life work.

Designing Effective Training Activities

Let's look at some creative and active training methods that address each of the three learning domains, cognitive (knowledge/thinking), behavioral (skill/acting), and affective (attitude/feeling).

These training methods encourage learners to think for themselves, to question and speculate, to be self-directed and take responsibility for their own learning. They give trainees a simulated experience of doing the job within a protected context. And they involve the trainee emotionally. With all these methods, trainees are more likely to retain the information because they've discovered it for themselves.

Learning by Thinking

Within any job or task there is a certain amount of information the trainee has to know. The trainer needs to arouse interest in and stimulate questions about this information. If it's a diagram or form, using one-way communication to explain it or describe how to fill it out won't engage the trainee. Instead, provoke a self-directed inquiry using a simple worksheet such as that shown in Figure 4.5.

Figure 4.5 Self-Directed Inquiry Worksheet

Questions	Speculations

The purpose of the worksheet is to prompt the learner, who is already in an active and searching mode, to let natural curiosity stir questions and then speculate on answers before you share the information he or she needs.

For example, consider a requisition form. Most forms look more simple than they are. They have their own unique language, complete with abbreviations, acronyms, and other jargon, and accompanying instructions often give scant clarification. Ask the trainee to study the requisition form and use the worksheet to record questions and ideas about it. Now discuss what the trainee wrote on the worksheet. In this way you reinforce what the trainee already knows or thinks, and you answer questions or clarify misunderstandings.

Another means of engaging the trainee cognitively is an individualized variation of the Information Search to be described in Chapter 9. The trainer prepares a worksheet highlighting key information the trainee needs to know and gives it to the trainee along with the source(s) of the information. The trainee searches out the information in the resource material, using the worksheet as a guide. This method is particularly useful on matters of product or service knowledge, where the worksheet requires the trainee to identify features and benefits of products and services by drawing on information in company brochures and fact sheets.

Still another effective method of communicating cognitive information is *guided teaching* (Silberman 1990), an approach that uses the Socratic method of teaching. Instead of telling or explaining the material to the trainee, the trainer helps the trainee "discover" the information by asking a series of open-ended, content-related questions designed to help the trainee draw on his or her intuitive knowledge or actual experience.

Learning by Doing

Behavioral learning or skill development, of course, is acquired through hands-on application in an actual work situation. but it's often helpful to conduct one or more trial runs before trying it out on the job. In some situations role play can be very effective. Let's return to our customer service scenario. To give the trainee an opportunity to practice skills in dealing with an irate customer, the trainer sets the scene and assumes the role of the customer while the trainee plays the customer service representative. After the role play, the trainer gives the trainee feedback, citing specific examples of what the trainee did well and offering suggestions for improvement.

Learning by Caring

One type of learning often overlooked in OJT involves the affective learning domain—the area of feelings and attitudes. This type of learning is particularly important for those who are being retrained because learning new ways involves change and often creates fear and anxiety—powerful emotions that must be considered and addressed in the training plan. Let's take safety training, for example. Many workers believe workplace safety is a responsibility assigned to the safety department. In an OJT situation, the trainer must instill in the trainee a sense of personal responsibility for creating and maintaining a safe work environment. This includes not only responsibility for preventing accidents but also for eliminating near-misses. Helping employees take ownership of workplace safety is not easy. The effective trainer takes the learner through some what-if scenarios of potential safety violations and asks the trainee not only what he or she can do to prevent them, but also what the *personal* impact would be if the employee didn't take those measures. When workers embrace and commit to the philosophy that "safety is everybody's business," then the trainer has successfully met the affective learning objective.

In a customer-service context, one way to heighten trainee awareness is a reverse role play in which the trainer plays the rude or indifferent customer service representative and the trainee acts as the customer. The activity helps the trainee feel what it's like to be in the customer's shoes. At the end, the trainer conducts a brief discussion with the trainee about how he or she felt and what the trainee can do to prevent customers from having such a negative experience.

Teaching and Job Aids

When developing the instructional plan, be sure to include teaching and job aids. Teaching aids offer several approaches to explaining a concept or the details of a specific task. As you read in Chapter 2, people's learning styles differ. The greater the number of approaches you use, the greater the likelihood that your training efforts will pay off. Adults learn more easily and retain more when the material is framed for them and linked to knowledge they already have. Outlines and checklists are ideal for presenting information concisely. Guided notetaking (Silberman and Lawson 1995) is a popular technique for helping trainees capture important information. Give the trainee a handout that outlines major points but leave some portions blank, for the trainee to fill in. This technique is particularly helpful for those people who have difficulty knowing what to write down. Simple and uncluttered graphics also provide a framework for learning new material.

According to a study conducted by the University of Minnesota and 3M, when visuals are added to an oral presentation, the presentation becomes 43 percent more persuasive (Vogel et al. 1986). Research also shows that people retain 10 percent of what they hear, but 50 percent of what they hear *and* see. Although human beings process information through a variety and combination of perceptual modalities, more adults take in and process information visually than through any other means. Eighty-three percent of all learning begins through the eyes (Green 1984). Other studies show that a trainee retains only 15 percent of the spoken or written word, 30 percent if the trainee sees what's being done, and 75 percent when a procedure is described during a demonstration (Whitmore 1992). Think about

Figure 4.6 Principles of Quality Service

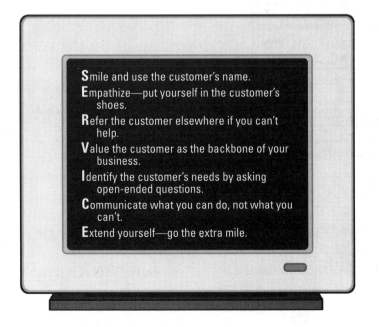

Smile and use the customer's name.
Empathize—put yourself in the customer's shoes.
Refer the customer elsewhere if you can't help.
Value the customer as the backbone of your business.
Identify the customer's needs by asking open-ended questions.
Communicate what you can do, not what you can't.
Extend yourself—go the extra mile.

the implications for the design and delivery of on-the-job training!

A job aid is documentation that provides the steps, illustration, or examples to use in performing a job correctly. It's especially useful for procedure changes or for tasks that are seldom done. Checklists, procedures manuals, on-line help screens, and reference cards are some common examples. When you created the job/task analysis chart earlier in this chapter, you created a job aid. Beyond serving as a leave-behind tutorial or reminder for the worker to use on an as-needed basis, job aids also function as teaching tools for OJT. Figure 4.6 is an example of a computer screen saver for use by a new customer service representative. Periodically popping up on the screen, it reminds the workers how the job should be done and reinforces the basic principles of delivering quality service.

Software, hardware, and equipment vendors often include job aids in their training packages or as optional support materials available at a nominal fee. Figure 4.7 is a job aid that speeds the keyboard operator working with an unfamiliar word-processing program.

Figure 4.7 An Example of a Job Aid

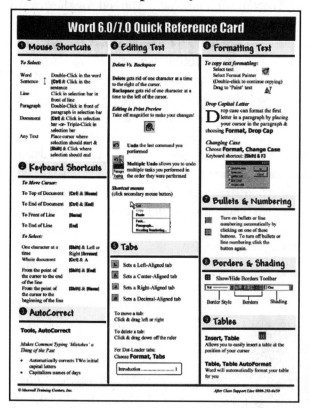

You may opt to create the job aids yourself, but consider asking the person currently doing the job to develop the aid. Who knows the job better? If more than one person performs the same task, form a committee to develop aids for various tasks.

Reprinted with permission from Maxwell Training Centers, Inc., Norristown, PA.

Chapter 5
Conducting the Training

Chapter Objectives:
▶ Create a safe and positive climate in which to conduct on-the-job training
▶ Prepare both the trainer and trainee for the training experience
▶ Use a structured, systematic approach to individualized training
▶ Involve others as resources and ongoing training support

Planning and Preparing to Train

Now it's time for pretraining preparation. Before you begin the actual instruction, the learning climate needs attention; both the trainer and the trainee have to prepare themselves for the work; and the training site, materials, and equipment must be readied for the training to begin.

Creating a Climate of Trust and Positive Expectations

The learning climate is a critical factor, particularly in one-on-one training. How you plan and prepare sets the tone for the entire process. Human beings are naturally motivated to learn but the entire issue of emotion cannot be overlooked. An adult's emotional state during the learning experience will affect how he or she will behave in the future (Wlodkowski 1993). Feelings, regarded as "chief movers" of behavior (Tomkins 1970), are an important aspect of adult learning.

Abraham Maslow places special emphasis on the role of safety in the learning process. He believes that human beings have two sets of needs—one that strives for growth and one that clings to safety. Safety is an important component to address in creating an environment that meets the learner's emotional needs. Trainers must create a climate of trust, openness, security, supportiveness, and mutual respect.

According to Maslow, "growth takes place when the next step forward is subjectively more delightful, more joyous, more intrinsically satisfying than the previous gratification with which we have become familiar and even bored…" (Maslow 1968). Both growth and safety have anxieties and delights, but we grow forward only "when the delights of growth and anxieties of safety are greater than the anxieties of growth and the delights of safety…" (Maslow 1968).

In other words, safety needs are stronger than growth needs.

The trainer is the key to satisfying these safety needs. Accepting, supportive, and empathetic trainer behavior establishes a safe environment. Because significant learning is often threatening, the trainer must provide an accepting and supportive climate with a heavy reliance on trainee responsibility. The trainer is a partner in the training process, expediting learning through a wide range of resources and techniques. This partnership concept is critical to learning for we cannot teach anyone anything directly; a person learns only what he or she sees as relevant.

People feel ready and eager to learn when they feel safe in the learning environment. This safety involves a high degree of trust—trust in the worth of the instructional design as well as in the competence of the instructor. If the participant sees little or no value in what is taught, the transfer of learning from instructional setting to real-world practice will be minimal (Robinson and Robinson 1989).

Trust is created by a sequence of events that advances from easier to more complex tasks. Participants learn to trust and feel safe when they are given an opportunity to express themselves without being judged (Vella 1994). They must feel comfortable to ask questions and make mistakes without feeling stupid or inadequate. Here we should consider the Pygmalion effect, the principle of the self-fulfilling prophecy. People will perform according to what is expected of them, either positively or negatively. The power of expectation alone can influence the behavior of others. To put it another way, one's expectations about a future event affect the likelihood that it will happen just that way. The Pygmalion effect can surely influence a trainee's success. A trainer can easily communicate positive or negative expectations to the trainee through inadvertent verbal and nonverbal messages. If a trainer says, "Give it a shot" in a tone of voice that says, "I don't expect much from you," there is a great likelihood the trainee will perform accordingly and accomplish little. When we communicate to others our high expectations of them, their self-confidence grows, their capabilities develop, and their accomplishments multiply.

Preparing the Trainer

As a trainer, you need to be mentally prepared for the experience. Begin with information about the trainee. Find out as much as you can beforehand. Read the new employee's resume or job application. Talk to a current employee's supervisor. Although you've developed a structured training plan to ensure consistency and thoroughness, you'll want to tailor your approach to fit the trainee's skill and experience level, individual learning style, and personal needs. Talk to the trainee yourself and/or ask him or her to complete a pretraining questionnaire designed to elicit information about previous job and instructional experiences. The more you know about the trainee, the better. The answers to the following questions will help you personalize a standard instructional plan to match the trainee each time you deliver a new training.

➡ Who is the trainee?

➡ What does the trainee need to know?

➡ How much does the trainee already know?

➡ What are the trainee's goals?

Preparing the Trainee

All training should be placed in context. Before training begins, show the trainee the "big picture." Focus on how the task or knowledge fits into the job as a whole and even how the job fits into the bigger department or organization picture. What may be obvious to you as trainer may not be so obvious to the trainee. Also explain why a task has to be done a certain way or within a particular time frame. As Malcolm Knowles (1990) says, adults "have a deep need to know why they need to know something before they are willing to invest the time and energy in learning it"—even when it's clearly part of the job.

To reflect adult learning principles, the training should build on existing knowledge. Adults come to the workplace and the training arena with a range of experience. Let's take computer experience, as an example. At one end of the spectrum, you have an employee who knows no more than how to withdraw cash from an automated teller machine. At the other end, you have a skilled hacker. Between those polar opposites are all your other workers.

One key to successful training is to start where the trainee *is,* not where you want him or her to be. To discover your starting point, avoid self-limiting queries like, "Do you know how to use a computer?" Ask open-ended questions such as, "What computer experience have you had?" Along the same subject lines you might use the following questions to uncover a trainee's knowledge and skill level:

➡ How long have you used a computer?

➡ What have you used a computer for?

➡ What type of computer have you used?

➡ How did you learn to use a computer?

Although you may have asked similar questions on a pretraining questionnaire, this more personal, face-to-face needs assessment will go a long way in creating a comfortable training environment.

After you've determined the trainee's skill level, express your confidence in the trainee's ability and explain that mistakes are both predictable and okay. Tell the trainee that it's most important for the two of you to find out why he or she made the mistake, how to correct it, and how to prevent it from happening in the future. Always be enthusiastic and accentuate the positive by emphasizing the rewards of learning, not the penalties or disadvantages of *not* learning. Another important guideline to communicate is that it's often more critical for the trainee to know where to find information than to *know* the information.

Preparing the Training Site

No matter how difficult, it's crucial to set aside a time for training that is as free from interruptions as possible. Minimize distractions by asking others to screen phone calls, and try to make the setting physically and aesthetically comfortable. Be sure to sit or stand next to the trainee. Sitting side by side, both of you experience the task or the use of equipment from the same physical perspective. And where you position yourself contributes to the relationship you are trying to build with the trainee. Sitting side by side creates a friendly, open environment that encourages two-way communication.

OJT implies that the training will take place at the actual work station. Equipment and supplies are probably in place, but check to see that equipment is in working order and that you have all the teaching aids and reference manuals on hand. Also make sure there are sufficient materials for practice. Arrange the materials neatly in their order of use. Create examples of completed work, and provide trainer notes, aids, and resources.

Presenting the Training

Throughout the training process, remember that learning is personal and individual. The effective trainer uses a variety of methods to ensure interaction and communication with all types of people. Remember that you need to address all three learning domains: Thinking, acting and feeling.

📖 CASE STUDY: Computer Training

The following case study briefly illustrates the training process, including the eight-step procedural model. Jan is training recently hired Doug in how to use a computer.

Jan: Hi, Doug. Are you ready to get started?

Doug: I guess so.

Jan: Good. First of all, what experience have you had with computers?

Find out what trainee knows

Doug: Not much. I've watched my kids use one, but I've never tried one myself.

Jan: Well, computers can be quite intimidating at first. I remember the first time I sat in front of a computer screen. I was scared to death. I thought for sure I was going to blow up something, or at the very least hit the wrong key and erase all the information. I was completely computer illiterate, so if I can learn, anyone can. First of all, we're going to focus on getting you comfortable with some basic word processing. By the end of the first week, you'll be able to write basic letters and reports using the PC with little or no help from me or the manual.

Reassure trainee

Tell trainee what to expect

Doug: I'm not so sure.

Jan: Trust me. Okay, first of all, sit right down here in front of the computer. Let's turn it on and get started…now why don't you tell me what you think the various keys are for.

STEP ONE: Speculation

(Doug points out the obvious keys but shows that he's baffled by the function keys.)

> Doug, I'd like you just to watch me as I hit some of these keys and see what happens on the screen. I'm not going to explain anything right now. I just want you to watch….

Many OJT situations involve hands-on, task-specific applications or procedures, and it's important to have a model for doing any type of procedural training. As noted earlier, the traditional approach was a four-step process developed during World War I and modified to seven steps during World War II. The process typically involves planning and preparing, presenting the operation (tell, show, explain, and demonstrate), giving the trainee the opportunity to perform the operation, and conducting appropriate follow up. A more active approach offers an eight-step model that involves the trainee more directly in the process. This model expands and enhances how the trainer presents the operation. Moving from a trainer-centered approach in which the trainee is passive while the trainer tells, shows, explains, and demonstrates, the following eight-step protocol reflects and incorporates what we know about adult learning, motivation, and learning styles. For a real-life view of this training model, read the Case Study below.

STEP TWO: Observation
(Jan performs the task while Doug watches.)

    Okay, now I'm going to hit the same keys again and I'll explain exactly what they do.

STEP THREE: Explanation
(Jan explains the function keys and various commands.)

    Now, Doug, I'm going to show you step-by-step how to set up a letter, using the various keys I just explained.

STEP FOUR: Demonstration
(Jan demonstrates the process.)

What questions and observations do you have about what I just demonstrated?

Doug: I really don't have any questions right now. It seems pretty simple.

Jan: What I would like you to do now, Doug, is to pretend you are the trainer and I am the student. Tell me how I should go about writing a letter on the computer. I'll follow your instructions.

STEP FIVE: Role Reversal
(Doug instructs Jan in how to set margins, use the function keys, delete characters, change fonts, and so forth. She follows his directions.)

    Good. Now I want you to prepare this letter for me, and I'll just sit here in case you have any questions or run into any problems.

STEP SIX: Performance
(Jan gives Doug a handwritten letter.)

    Good. You really seem to be getting the hang of it. How do you feel?

Doug: Well, I feel more comfortable than I did an hour ago.

Jan: I hope so. I think you're ready to move on to envelopes. But before we do that, here are some more letters I'd like you to practice doing just to make sure you'll be able to do them on your own. If you run into any problems, just let me know. In any case, I'll check back with you in an hour to see how you're doing.

STEP SEVEN: Practice
STEP EIGHT: Monitor and Follow-up

An Eight-Step Training Protocol

1. Arouse curiosity and prompt speculation.
2. Perform the task silently.
3. Describe the task and place it in context.
4. Perform and explain the task, step by step.
5. Exchange roles with the trainee.
6. Observe the trainee's performance and give feedback.
7. Let the trainee practice independently.
8. Conduct periodic checks and monitor progress.

Step One: Speculation

Human beings are naturally curious. We all possess internal motives that can be channeled effectively into educational pursuits. Intrinsic sources of motivation include curiosity, competence, and identification. We are attracted by what is unclear or uncertain, and as we search for and achieve clarity, we experience satisfaction, which then promotes further curiosity. At the same time, we're driven to reach competence. We develop interest in areas where we achieve or excel. We also identify with people we respect and whose respect we want, and we subscribe to their standards. In this first step, arouse the trainee's curiosity and help him or her establish a frame of reference for the actual training that will follow. Take advantage of natural motivation by asking the trainee to guess how to do the task or procedure or about the particular things that should be considered when completing the task.

Step Two: Observation

Have the learner watch as you perform the entire task. Don't explain or answer any questions during this step. The learner is to focus attention *visually* on the task at hand. When people try to watch and listen at the same time, their concentration is diluted. After you've completed the demonstration, ask the trainee to explain what you did. If you have more than one trainee, ask them to work in pairs and discuss what they saw, then share their observations with you and the rest of the group. If a trainee has difficulty understanding your demonstration of the task or procedure, repeat the process.

Step Three: Explanation

To reinforce the visual presentation, now explain the task or procedure, giving an overview of the entire job. Explain the reason(s) for doing the task and how it fits into the big picture, including other people or departments that will be affected. This step provides a framework by addressing both the *what* and *why*. Once again, the trainee's attention will be concentrated on one perceptual modality, the aural.

Step Four: Demonstration

In a step-by-step manner, show how the task is done, stressing key points along the way. Here you combine aural and visual as the trainee listens and watches you perform the work. The difference between this and Step Two is that you are now proceeding more slowly and methodically. Check for understanding by asking open-ended questions as you demonstrate. Don't ask, "Do you understand?" because that will elicit only a yes or no response. (Most likely yes, either because the trainee believes he understands what you're doing or because she's afraid to admit she doesn't understand.) Questions that start with *What* or *How* are very effective in discovering whether the trainee truly understands the procedure.

Step Five: Role Reversal

This step offers an interesting twist to the procedural training model. When you're comfortable with the trainee's level of understanding, switch roles. Ask the trainee to become the trainer for this step. You follow the trainee's instructions on how to perform the work. If the trainee directs you incorrectly, either do the task as instructed and use the resulting negative consequence as a learning tool, or stop and explain why the instruction is incorrect and what could result from that action. It's an added plus that people are likely to master what they teach.

Step Six: Performance

Ask the trainee to perform the operation while you watch. As needed, correct mistakes on the fly to prevent reinforcing bad habits. Be sure to give specific feedback and positive reinforcement. Don't just say, "Good job!" Tell the person exactly what he or she is doing well. If the trainee has not quite mastered the task, be patient and avoid critical, sarcastic, or demeaning comments such as "I can't believe you're having such a hard time with this" or "Everyone else I've trained has grasped this right away." Be very careful in how you speak to your trainees. No matter what their knowledge or skill level, your trainees are adults and will resent being talked down to or treated like children. Also be careful not to communicate a negative reaction through nonverbal signals. Sighing or rolling your eyes can be just as damaging as negative words.

Step Seven: Practice

Once you are confident that the trainee can perform the task and understands the reason for it, let the trainee practice alone. Encourage the trainee to ask questions and seek any necessary help. Offer words of assurance and encouragement and say that you'll be checking back periodically. This step is vital because it helps the trainee become comfortable with the task by letting him or her make mistakes without the pressure of the trainer's critical eye.

Step Eight: Monitor and Evaluate

When the trainee has mastered the task, what remains is continued development of confidence and competency. Conduct several progress checks, gradually tapering them off. Monitor the trainee's progress by observing performance and asking open-ended questions. Ultimately, you will measure results against performance standards and objectives, as we'll discuss in Chapter 6.

Turn to Action Item 5.1 and outline a training plan following these eight steps.

Involving Other Employees as Resources

Shared Departmental Training

Keeping people up to date and fresh on products, procedures, and techniques is always difficult. As we have noted earlier, supervisors and designated trainers often have multiple responsibilities that pull them in several directions at the same time and make it impossible to handle all the follow-up questions that come their way. One solution is to enlist the help of all staff members, from the newcomer to the veteran. For example, if your business requires employees to know about products and services, create "product specialists." Assign a product or service to each person. Ask individuals to learn everything about their assignment. Hold regularly scheduled department training meetings and ask these specialists to take turns briefing the staff about their area of expertise. When employees have questions or need help, they can go to the specialist for answers and support. This approach relieves some pressure and stress from the supervisor because he or she won't repeatedly be interrupted by employees with routine questions. People needing help won't have to wait to catch the manager's attention. And those des-

---

⚡ *ACTION ITEM 5.1* ⚡

Choose a task or procedure and outline how you would go about presenting it to an employee.

Name of task/procedure:_____

Name of trainee: _____

What you know about trainee's experience/skill level relative to this task?

_____

_____

Questions you might ask to find out more about trainee's knowledge, experience, skill level:

_____

_____

Materials/equipment needed for training:

_____

Step One: Speculation—questions to arouse trainee's curiosity about the task or procedure:

_____

_____

Step Two: Observation—how you are going to demonstrate the task:

_____

_____

Step Three: Explanation—what you are going to explain (include key terms, the big picture, and so forth):

_____

_____

ignated as specialists not only develop skill in presentation and coaching but also experience a greater sense of self-worth and increased job satisfaction.

Managers and supervisors can develop ongoing departmental training sessions to keep staff members up on new trends, and techniques or to help them fine-tune such skills as selling or customer service. Role plays are particularly effective in this type of group training. Bringing in guest speakers from time to time is also useful. You may want to start a type of intramural speakers bureau in which representatives from various departments help paint the big picture by attending other departments' training sessions to tell them about what their departments do. This is particularly effective in creating a team spirit throughout the organization.

It's critical that we see learning as an active endeavor. The more we involve the learner, the more he or she will learn. To that end, the trainer must create an environment conducive to learning and approach training as a process of two-way communication.

Step Four: Demonstration—outline the step-by-step procedure:

_____

_____

Open-ended questions to check for understanding:

_____

_____

Step Five: Role Reversal—how you are going to present the role reversal and what you are going to be looking for from the trainee:

_____

_____

Step Six: Performance—what you expect the trainee to demonstrate to you:

_____

Step Seven: Practice—what you are going to have the trainee practice and how much time you are going to allot:

_____

Standard of performance:

_____

Step Eight: Monitor and Evaluate—when you will check back with the trainee:

_____

Open-ended questions to ask during follow-up:

_____

_____

Chapter 6
Evaluating and Transferring Training

Chapter Objectives:
▶ Develop and use tools to evaluate training effectiveness on four levels
▶ Develop follow-up processes to ensure transfer of training

VIGNETTE 6.1 START WORRYING

*K*azim *had just finished his on-the-job training with Kim, his OJT instructor. Over the past few weeks, he has frequently asked Kim for feedback on his performance, and Kim's reply has always been the same: "Stop worrying, Kazim. You're doing fine." But now the moment of truth has arrived. Kazim will be completely on his own tomorrow and he isn't confident that he can handle all the customers' questions and demands by himself. Doubts run through his mind: "What if I give out the wrong information? What will I do if a customer has a problem I've never encountered? What happens if I enter the wrong information in the computer?"*

Does the situation described here sound familiar? Have you or anyone you've trained experienced the same self-doubt and insecurity because there was no tangible indicator of what the trainee has learned or how well the trainer prepared the employee?

Who Cares About Evaluation?

Learners, especially adults, need to know how they are doing and need to be reassured that they are making satisfactory progress. The trainer also needs to know how he or she is doing in preparing trainees to perform their jobs. Managers need some way to measure the effectiveness of the training and both the trainer's and the trainee's performances. For it to be meaningful, the evaluation process must begin even before the employee receives training. The criteria for measuring training success are determined by the specific standards of performance and various metrics that the manager or someone else in the organization has established at the outset. These criteria, of course, are linked to specific business needs and priorities.

The Four Levels of Evaluation
✔ Reaction—Evaluating the trainer
✔ Learning—Evaluating the trainee's comprehension and retention
✔ Behavior—Evaluating the trainee's transfer of training to the job
✔ Results—Evaluating OJT's impact on business goals and outcomes

Levels of Evaluation

The classic model of evaluation put forth by Donald Kirkpatrick (1994) comprises four levels: Reaction, learning, behavior, and results. By looking at evaluation from these four perspectives we can address the who, what, when, why, and how of the evaluation and measurement process. All perspectives are important and no level should be by-passed.

Level One: Reaction

Let's start with the easiest and most common level of evaluation—trainee reaction. At this fundamental level, the trainer solicits formal feedback from the trainee to help determine the training's effectiveness and how it can be improved. Many trainers dismiss as unimportant these so-called "smile sheets." Some regard them as merely popularity indicators that contribute little to the evaluation process. Kirkpatrick sees Level One as particularly important because "if they [trainees] do not react favorably, they will not be motivated to learn" (Kirkpatrick 1994).

One way to measure trainer effectiveness is to develop a questionnaire (Figure 6.1) for both the trainer and the learner to complete at the end of the training period (Lawson 1994). The questionnaire compares perceptions and uncovers communication problems that may be sabotaging the training efforts. Level One evaluation addresses the design, delivery, instruction, training site, perceived learning, and the trainee's level of satisfaction with the training experience. When creating a reaction questionnaire, be sure to design questions to assess the trainer's effectiveness in the following areas:

➡ climate setting

➡ conducting the training

➡ reinforcing the training

➡ communicating.

The questionnaire is a way for each trainee to offer specific and meaningful feedback to the trainer as a means of improving the trainer's effectiveness. It also helps the trainee to reflect on the formal OJT process and register his or her degree of satisfaction with it. The questionnaire can also yield valuable information to the trainer's manager who can use the data as supporting documentation for the manager's evaluation of the trainer's performance. This type of questionnaire should be used at several times throughout the training process, not merely at the end.

Level Two: Learning

Level Two evaluation deals with what is learned, the knowledge and skills the trainees retain. It addresses the trainee's demonstrated mastery of the principles, facts, techniques, and skills presented in the formal training. Evaluation of and feedback concerning the trainee's progress should be an ongoing process, both formally and informally.

Figure 6.1 Reaction Questionnaire

Trainer Effectiveness

Trainer's Name: _____   Check one: _____ Trainer's Self-Evaluation
Trainee's Name: _____   _____ Trainee's Feedback

Instructions: Please evaluate the instructor's effectiveness by placing a checkmark in the appropriate column.

	Excellent	Good	Fair	Poor
	4	3	2	1

How effective was the trainer in...?

		Excellent	Good	Fair	Poor
1.	Arranging the work area as it should be.	____	____	____	____
2.	Providing necessary supplies and materials.	____	____	____	____
3.	Putting the trainee at ease.	____	____	____	____
4.	Explaining what to expect.	____	____	____	____
5.	Asking the trainee about his/her experience, knowledge, and interests.	____	____	____	____
6.	Explaining how the task fits into the big picture.	____	____	____	____
7.	Explaining the complete task clearly.	____	____	____	____
8.	Demonstrating the task step-by-step.	____	____	____	____
9.	Explaining the reason for each step.	____	____	____	____
10.	Having the trainee explain and perform subtasks.	____	____	____	____
11.	Asking open-ended questions to check understanding.	____	____	____	____
12.	Offering specific and frequent feedback.	____	____	____	____
13.	Correcting mistakes constructively.	____	____	____	____
14.	Keeping the trainee interested and involved.	____	____	____	____
15.	Demonstrating patience and understanding.	____	____	____	____
16.	Providing written procedures and/or job aids.	____	____	____	____
17.	Using easily understood language, terms, and examples.	____	____	____	____
18.	Giving positive reinforcement.	____	____	____	____
19.	Giving trainee opportunities to practice.	____	____	____	____
20.	Monitoring progress regularly.	____	____	____	____

Subtotal ____

TOTAL ____

Suggestions for improvement:

_____
_____
_____

Several methods can and should be used to evaluate the trainee's skill and knowledge of the job, task, or procedures that he or she is expected to perform. First of all, the trainer can watch the trainee performing the task during the initial training period, taking notes and providing feedback. Another method is to track various predetermined metrics such as number of errors, length of time to complete a task, measurable outputs, and so forth.

Periodic testing is another option. Any formal testing should be kept simple: Short quizzes at day's end or some type of take-home assignment. It may be appropriate to give both a pretest and a posttest to measure the impact of training. Developing test or quiz questions is not an easy task. They can be either subjective (e.g., short answer or essay) or objective (e.g., multiple-choice or true-false). When writing questions, consider your trainee's learning style, the time needed to grade the tests, and both the validity and reliability of each item. Above all else, remember that a question should assess the learning specified in the training and test only those skills directly related to the objective. Rather than asking for simple recall of information, such as definitions, ask questions that require trainees to apply or interpret what they've learned.

In most cases you will probably choose to develop multiple choice questions. If so, make sure you follow these guidelines:

➡ Avoid "all of the above" and "none of the above" in your set of answer options.

➡ Make sure the stem (i.e., the main part of the question) contains most of the information and defines the problem, and place missing words near the end.

➡ Maintain grammatical consistency or parallel structure for both the stem and the answer choices.

➡ Try to create answer choices of equal length.

➡ Avoid ambiguity and reading difficulty by stating questions in the positive rather than in the negative.

Informal Feedback

As we've noted, adult learners want and need to know how they're doing, both formally and informally. An informal evaluation is generally based on observation of the trainee's performance during the training period. Like any other feedback, it should be delivered in private immediately following the observed behavior. The purpose isn't only to comment on the employee's performance, but also to encourage open, two-way communication. When informal feedback is handled haphazardly, with seemingly little thought or caring, it can have very serious consequences.

Read the Case Study on page 53 and jot down how the supervisor might have done a better job of giving the trainee feedback about his performance.

📖 CASE STUDY: What Went Wrong?

Sam Lopez supervised a refrigeration manufacturer's distribution department. With his recent promotion to this position he inherited a number of experienced workers and one new employee, Jeremy Taylor, who'd been onboard for a week.

It was the end of the month and Sam was under a lot of pressure to get the inventory out of the warehouse, loaded onto trucks, and on the road to customers. Loading the large refrigeration units was hard work but not difficult, and because he saw Jeremy just following around one of the other workers and watching, Sam decided to assign Jeremy to work on the loading dock.

> "Jeremy, come over here!" Sam yelled on his way to check on inventory control. "Listen, these units need to go on the truck, pronto! The customer expected them last week, and we're gonna lose money if we don't get them out of here today. Do you think you can handle it?"
>
> "Sure, boss. No problem," said Jeremy.
>
> At the end of the day, Sam stopped Jeremy on his way out the door and asked, "Did you get all those units loaded? Any problems?"
>
> "They're probably halfway across the state by now. Everything went fine. See ya tomorrow."

Sam was relieved and thought to himself, "This guy's gonna work out great. At least that's one headache I won't have to worry about."

> A few days later, Sam called Jeremy into his office and began shouting at him. "I thought you told me everything went fine with those units you loaded!" Without waiting for a response, he continued, "Well, let me tell you that everything was *not* fine. When the truck arrived on the customer's doorstep, almost all the units were damaged. You didn't load them nice and tight and so they banged into each other along the way. Now the company's out a lot of money and I'm in hot water, thanks to you."
>
> "I don't understand it, Sam," responded Jeremy. "I got 'em on the truck and out the door in record time. You said so yourself. What happened?"
>
> "I'll tell you what happened. You didn't put the shorter boxes in the narrow end of the truck with the larger ones up against them. How could you do that? Anyone with half a brain would know to do that. It's common sense. You can bet this is going to show up on your personnel record and if anything like this happens again, you're out of here. Now get back to work."

Clearly, Sam did many things wrong. He didn't clearly define the performance expectations, nor did he create checkpoints or observe Jeremy's performance. He should have told Jeremy that he was to load they units so that they would not move during transit. He should have explained that if the units were not loaded tightly, much of the merchandise would be damaged and the company would suffer a significant financial loss. Furthermore, Sam should have told Jeremy to load the shorter boxes in the narrow end of the truck with the larger ones behind and he should have checked Jeremy's work fairly early on to see if he was meeting the standards set. Sam handled the feedback session badly, too. He was judgmental and made personal attacks on Jeremy. There was certainly no evidence of any attempt at two-way communication or at helping to improve Jeremy's performance.

Formal Progress Checks

Because the designated trainer and supervisor have their own jobs at the same time that someone is being trained, most evaluation and feedback is done informally. However, a weekly progress report will help all parties measure training and learning efforts along the way. The report presented in Figure 6.2 is brief but prompts and documents a continuous assessment.

Figure 6.2 Weekly Progress Report

Week ending: _____ Trainee's Name: _____

Position: _____ Trainer's Name: _____

Performance Levels:
   1—All aspects of task performed correctly; standards met consistently
   2—Most aspects of task performed correctly; standards met somewhat
   3—Few aspects of task performed correctly; does not meet standards

Task: _____ Performance Level: _____
    Comments: _____
    Goal: _____
Task: _____ Performance Level: _____
    Comments: _____
    Goal: _____
Task: _____ Performance Level: _____
    Comments: _____
    Goal: _____
Task: _____ Performance Level: _____
    Comments: _____
    Goal: _____

Whether formal or informal, an evaluation of a trainee's performance should address the following areas:

➡ Job knowledge

➡ Performance standards (quality, quantity, speed, accuracy)

➡ Strengths

➡ Specific areas for improvement

➡ Action plan

Figure 6.3 Trainee Evaluation for Bank Teller

Trainee's Name:_____ **Position:** _____

Trainer: _____ **Date:**_____

Competency Scores:

4 Outstanding	Outstanding performer; exceeds expectations; requires little or no supervision
3 Above Standards	Performs above expectations; requires some supervision or direction
2 Meets Standards	Meets standards of performance; requires expected level of supervision
1 Below Standards	Performs below standards and expectations; requires considerable supervision and guidance

Part I: Job Knowledge

A. Products and Services _____ Score
    Comments: _____

    _____

B. Organizational Policies _____ Score
    Comments: _____

    _____

C. Security Procedures _____ Score
    Comments: _____

    _____

Part II: Processing Skills
Place competency score for each category and each skill in the appropriate box.

	Quality	Quantity	Accuracy	Speed
Check cashing				
Cash handling				
Withdrawals				
Deposits				
Loan payments				
Miscellaneous transactions				
Successful settlement				

Figure 6.3 Trainee Evaluation for Bank Teller (continued)

Part III: Customer Relations

A. Telephone Skills _____ Score

Comments: _____

_____

_____

B. Face-to-Face Interaction _____ Score

Comments: _____

_____

_____

Part IV: Developmental Plan

A. Strengths

1. List knowledge areas in which the trainee excels.

_____

_____

_____

2. List the skills in which the trainee excels.

_____

_____

_____

B. Specific Areas for Improvement

1. List knowledge areas in which trainee needs additional training.

_____

_____

_____

2. List specific skills that need improvement.

_____

_____

_____

C. Action Plan

_____

_____

_____

_____

_____

_____

Trainer's Signature _____ **Date** _____

Trainee's Signature _____ **Date** _____

Manager's Signature _____ **Date** _____

Figure 6.3 is an example of a formal evaluation tool that includes all five areas. This type of evaluation should be completed at the end of the training period. It's a good way to let the trainee know where he or she stands, and it also indicates what additional coaching or even remedial training may be needed.

Level Three: Behavior

The true test of the learner's mastery of skill or task is performance on the job, once again measured against established performance standards. Because people will do what they will be measured on, it is important to communicate standards and expectations clearly at the beginning and throughout the training process. To ensure the transfer of training to the work performed, the adult learner must be able to apply what he or she has learned within 24 hours.

Analysis of how well the skills have been applied to the actual job situation should be an ongoing process. First determine what skills are being used, any barriers preventing the transfer of training, and any perception gaps. Both hard and soft data should be collected. Soft data include interviews, focus groups, and on-site observation. Surveys sent to the employee, the employee's supervisor, and the employee's subordinates, if appropriate, also gather soft data. Hard data include work outputs and other operational results.

For interviews, who and how many people you interview depend on several factors: Time, cost, and availability of the interviewees. You should conduct structured interviews with the employee as well as his or her supervisor. In some cases, it may be appropriate to interview the employee's peers, subordinates, and even customers. Interview questions, limited to no more than 10, should be open-ended, using primarily questions that begin with "What" and "How."

Observation does not have to be conducted directly. For telephone customer service training, for example, Level Three information can be captured by taped interactions.

Documenting the transfer of training to the actual job situation is critical. One way to ensure that documentation is accurate and up-to-date is to create a performance checklist that lists all the tasks associated with a particular job and the metrics or standards of performance (Figure 6.4). The supervisor signs off on each item to indicate the employee knowledge and proficiency were satisfactory when observed.

A tool such as Figure 6.4 is particularly helpful for organizations seeking ISO 9000 certification. ISO 9000 is a set of five universal standards for a quality assurance system used worldwide. Required to document OJT, some organizations find themselves in a real predicament when they discover they have no system in place. The performance checklist also saves time when coupled with observation intended to access an employee's level of proficiency. It enables the trainer to focus on the activities with which the trainee is unfamiliar and not waste time on tasks the trainee knows how to do.

It is not enough to help adults learn new tasks or behaviors through training; adults must also be helped to apply those learned tasks or behaviors. Trainers can help ensure the trainee's successful application of skill and knowledge by connecting with the trainee periodically to uncover and address any trainee resistance.

An employee whose performance level is below expectations is sometimes stuck and seems to be unwilling or unable to change. By talking with the trainee, the trainer will often identify real or perceived barriers that are keeping the trainee from meeting perfor-

Figure 6.4 Performance Checklist for a Bank Teller

Supervisor's Initials _____ Date _____

Branch Operations

A. Security Procedures
   1. Knows branch opening procedures
   2. Knows locations of:
      —dye packs and transmitter
      —cameras or video
      —bait money and procedures
      —alarm and camera buttons
      —weekly fraud alerts
      —Knows teller terminal and cash drawer security
      —Knows robbery procedures
B. Basic Teller Procedures
   1. Performs basic computer skills
      —teller opening procedures
      —proof-cash count
      —computer keys
      —teller closing procedures
   2. Performs other teller procedures
      —counts cash accurately
      —proper use of coin counter
      —proper use of cash slips
      —check cutter
      —completes settlement sheet accurately
      —identifies proper signer on accounts
      —cash advance procedures
C. Processing Basic Transactions
   1. Uses speed keys
      —cash checks
      —deposits
      —cash-back deposits
      —credit line
      —cash withdrawals
      —check withdrawals
   2. Uses tran keys
      —loan payments
      —savings accounts
   3. Performs miscellaneous transactions
      —money order sales
      —traveler checks sales
      —bond sales
      —utility payments
      —safe deposit box payments
      —bond coupons

mance standards. Sometimes these barriers, such as competing time demands or discouragement from coworkers, are conditions beyond the trainee's control. Or internal barriers may be found, like poor work habits or lack of confidence. Confronted with barriers, the trainer needs to put on the coaching hat and help the trainee overcome any internal or external obstacles that make success unattainable.

Level Four: Results

Level Four evaluation, intended to measure the impact on the bottom line, is challenging. Measuring business results is difficult, expensive, and unreliable. This fourth level of evaluation demands a high degree of consistency in the design and delivery of OJT. Determining the effect of training on business generally applies to group or classroom training because greater numbers of workers are trained at once. It is possible, however, to measure specific quantifiable results, such as fewer processing errors, more units produced, fewer pieces of damaged equipment, fewer customer complaints, decreased materials costs, increased sales, and fewer safety violations. The outcomes must be linked to business goals that are set by senior management, communicated to the first-line supervisors, and in turn, communicated to individual employees.

✒ *ACTION ITEM 6.1* ✒

Use the following questions to develop an Action Plan:

✒ What one task or procedure will you target to apply the training skills you have learned in this book?

_____

✒ Who is the person to whom you will teach the particular task or procedure?

_____

✒ What obstacles might get in the way of your success in applying these training skills?

_____

_____

_____

✒ What strategies will you use to overcome these potential barriers?

_____

_____

_____

Ongoing Evaluation

Evaluating the trainee's success on the job should be done periodically and for at least three months following completion of the training. Once again, observation is an excellent method, with the trainer or supervisor using a checklist to indicate the trainee's level of performance.

Action Planning

For training to be effective, learners must be able to apply what they have learned to their work situation. This is also true for you, the supervisor or designated trainer. With that in mind, develop a plan detailing how you will apply what you have learned in this module to your work situation. Turn to Action Item 6.1.

Chapter 7
On-the-Job Coaching

Chapter Objectives:
- Identify the supervisor's role in the coaching process
- Learn how to coach to reinforce training
- Learn how to give meaningful and constructive feedback
- Appreciate the value of monitoring progress

Once the employee has learned the skills through the initial training, one might believe the job of training is complete. Not so! The next phase of the training cycle is on-the-job coaching, an ongoing process generally performed by the trainee's manager or supervisor. Peer coaching is also being used more frequently, particularly in team environments and especially within self-directed work teams. Coaching is a continual process designed to help the employee gain greater competence and overcome barriers to improving competency once he or she has the knowledge or skills to perform job tasks. Coaching encourages people to do more than they ever imagined they could and is appropriate when the person has the ability and knowledge to do the job but is not meeting performance expectations.

Poor Coaches:
✔ Have never been trained
✔ Don't value the time required to do it
✔ Don't have the patience
✔ Think the employee can sink or swim

Coaching is an important skill for any manager or supervisor who wants to develop peak performers. The sad truth, however, is that many managers and supervisors are poor coaches. To understand better how to create consummate coaches, we must begin by taking a look at managers' and supervisors' internal barriers that prevent them from developing their coaching skills:

They don't know how to coach. Most supervisors have received no training on how to coach. Many were promoted to their positions because they were good at what they did. In addition to their new responsibilities, someone sprinkles "magic dust" on them and *voila!* They are now supposed to know how to manage or supervise. Right? Wrong. Without formal training, supervisors are left to their own devices, managing and supervising through trial-and-error or modeling the behavior of managers and supervisors for whom they have worked. Quite likely, they were never coached along the way and, therefore, they have no clue how to do it.

They don't want to take the time to coach. No doubt about it, coaching takes time. The supervisors who say they don't have the time to coach also say they have no time to delegate but are constantly bemoaning the poor performance of their employees and their own overwhelming workload. Time management experts know that for every hour spent planning, three to four hours are saved in execution. The same principle holds true for coaching. Time spent coaching in the short term results in long-term benefits.

They don't have the patience to coach. Although it's true that some people are not patient by nature, they can develop patience by focusing on the positive outcomes of coaching and practicing it daily.

They believe the person should do it on his or her own. Many supervisors believe that because the employee has received the initial training, he or she can sink or swim alone. In some cases, the supervisor may have the attitude that says, "I had to learn it the hard way, and if I can do it, so can everyone else."

Coaching does take time. It involves real commitment and a desire to participate actively in an employee's development. Throughout the coaching process, it's important to keep in mind that the main objective is to improve performance. Supervisors shouldn't jump to early conclusions about an employee who might not be as competent with the new task or job as the supervisor expects. There may be other factors affecting the employee's performance, factors over which the worker has little or no control.

An important skill in the coaching process is the ability to offer encouragement. You can promote competence and confidence in others by encouraging them to stretch, acknowledge their own accomplishments, and strive to achieve their personal best. Point out their improvements in performance, no matter how small, especially when employees are beginning new tasks. As Goethe once said, "Correction does much, but encouragement more; encouragement after censure is as the sun after a shower."

There are two different types of coaching: Spontaneous, on-the-spot coaching and planned, formal coaching.

On-the-Spot Coaching

On-the-spot coaching takes place whenever an opportunity presents itself. One of the inherent dangers of immediate, on-the-spot coaching is the supervisor's natural tendency to take over and do the task for the employee instead of helping the worker learn to do it better. Let's take computer training as an example. An employee may be working independently with a new software program, having received formal OJT. At some point, the worker gets stuck, either forgetting something previously taught or being confronted with an unusual problem or application. When the employee asks the supervisor what to do, the supervisor says, "Move over and let me do it. I can do it quicker myself," instead of taking the time to coach the employee through the process.

Formal Coaching

As with OJT, before you begin on-the-job coaching you must be clear about your expectations. Otherwise, you cannot communicate them to someone else. Specific performance standards are critical. If you want the employee to answer the telephone within three rings, then you must be sure you have communicated those expectations clearly. If you want the employee to greet customers in a friendly manner, be specific as to what you want the employee to do or say.

Primary Feedback Topics:
✔ Specific behaviors
✔ Positive aspects of performance
✔ Improvement priorities

An effective coach must also be a good observer. Before you can give appropriate feedback to the employee about his or her performance, you must be able to observe it firsthand, not act on hearsay from the employee's coworkers. Observation should be an ongoing process. When you are observing an employee's performance, there may be many things going on, verbal as well as nonverbal, positive and negative. It is neither possible nor desirable to focus on everything at once. Therefore, as you observe, think about three primary areas as the basis for the feedback discussion.

➡ Focus on describing specific behavior—what the employee actually said or did—rather than a sweeping remark such as, "You are warm and friendly" or something widely judgmental like, "You come across as disorganized and unprepared." Instead, say something like, "When a customer sits down to open a new account, you frequently fumble through several drawers before locating the necessary forms."

➡ Emphasize positive aspects of the employee's performance as a way of reinforcing and encouraging that behavior to continue. For example, say, "When Mr. Smith shouted at you, you maintained good self-control and responded to him very professionally."

➡ Prioritize the behaviors the employee needs to improve. Too many areas for action at the same time will confuse the employee and dilute his or her efforts to improve specific work-related behavior. Focus on one or two issues at a time.

To hone your observation skills and practice focusing on these primary feedback areas, complete Action Item 7.1 on page 64.

As you observe an employee's performance, be sure to document exactly what the person does or says. Be as objective as possible, focusing on the person's behavior and not on your reaction to it or your evaluation of it.

Preparing for the Formal Coaching Session

A formal coaching session is not something that just happens. It takes preparation and planning, sometimes even rehearsal.

⭐ ACTION ITEM 7.1 ⭐

Select an employee who has learned a new task or skill and whose current level of performance needs improvement. This employee can be newly hired or one who has been with your organization for some time.

Name of employee: _____

Task or skill: _____

What does the employee say or do that you want to continue? _____
_____

What exactly does the employee do (or not do) that you want to be done differently?
_____
_____

What specific examples of these behaviors have you observed, and when did you make the observation(s)?_____
_____

By when do you expect the employee to show improvement or demonstrate a particular level of proficiency? _____
_____

What will be your standard of measurement? _____
_____

What other behavior(s) needs to be changed or improved? *Be specific and rank them in order of importance.* _____
_____
_____
_____

Identify the Coaching Focus

The next step is to identify the behavior for which coaching is needed. Compare the specific expectations or standards of competency to the employee's current performance. The gap between the desired and the actual performance levels is your coaching focus.

Determine the Cause of the Problem

Here is where a coach's analytical skills are critical. The coach collects data and analyzes it, trying to determine preliminarily what might be causing the unsatisfactory performance. One or more of several possibilities may surface.

➡ *Unclear expectations:* Does the employee clearly understand what is expected of him or her?

➡ *External obstacles:* Are there extenuating circumstances preventing the employee from doing his or her best? Possibilities might include lack of resources, unrealistic parameters, or too many other responsibilities.

➡ *Lack of proper training:* Has the employee been given the skills or knowledge to do the job?

➡ *Lack of innate ability:* Does the employee have the ability to do the job? Do we have a duck when we really need a cat? Sometimes the problem is that we simply have someone in the wrong job.

At this point your analysis of the problem may be little more than educated speculation. You will verify your preliminary findings and assumptions during the actual coaching session by using your questioning, listening, and feedback skills to help the employee increase the present level of performance.

To help you prepare further for the coaching session, ask yourself the following questions:

➡ *Does the employee know my expectations?* Be clear about what you want.

➡ *What obstacles are there to meeting those expectations?* Make sure the employee has the training and resources to do the job.

➡ *Does the employee have the ability to meet my expectations or standards of performance?* Be certain you have the right person in the right job.

Create a Coaching Climate

Coaching, like training, requires a safe and comfortable environment that encourages open, two-way communication. The same setting and seating arrangements we discussed in Chapter 5 apply here. Factors that can inhibit or enhance the creation of a good environment are the coach's own body language and nonverbal cues. If you want to show genuine interest, sit forward in your chair or lean forward if standing, and avoid nervous gestures such as playing with your glasses or tapping your pen. You can send the wrong messages by crossing your arms (indicating defensiveness) or leaning back to stretch with your hands behind your head (a demonstration of superiority). Not only should you be conscious of what you are communicating nonverbally, but also be attuned to your employee's nonverbal cues. If the person is fidgeting, there's a good chance that he or she is nervous and uncomfortable with the discussion.

Address the Problem With the Employee

Spend time establishing rapport and clearly stating the purpose for the coaching session. For example, after some friendly conversation you might say something like, "What I would like to discuss with you today is how I can help you be more effective in dealing with irate customers."

Identify for the employee the expectations or performance standards and how his or her work is not in line with them. You might state this in a way similar to the following model:

In my observation of your performance, I noticed that you…
> State your perception of the problem using specific examples gathered from observation of actual performance.

I understand that it must be difficult for you to…but as you learned in your initial training…
> Express empathy and understanding.

We expect you to…
> Restate/clarify your expectations.

Effective Coaches:

✔ Measure performance in precise, objective terms
✔ State expectations clearly
✔ Focus on the positive performance they want rather than the negative consequences
✔ Encourage self-assessment
✔ Ask open-ended questions
✔ Listen actively to what the employee says
✔ Offer help as the employee strives to improve
✔ Monitor progress

Remember that exceptional coaches communicate and measure performance in precise, objective terms. They specify speed (rate), quantity (number or amount), quality or accuracy (absence of errors), thoroughness (completeness), and timeliness (meets deadlines) as illustrated below:

➡ "The expectation is that you will assemble an average of 100 widgets (quantity) per hour (rate) with zero defects (quality)."

➡ "We expect you to balance 100 percent of the time (accuracy) within 15 minutes (timeliness)."

➡ "I expect you to provide information for every line item (thoroughness) and submit this form three days before the end of the month (timeliness)."

Furthermore, effective coaches focus on the positive performance they want rather than the negative consequences. If the manager or supervisor has not clearly stated the expectations, the employee makes the assumption that standards really don't matter.

Feedback: The Essence of Coaching

Central to the coaching process is giving feedback. When done correctly, feedback is a valuable tool to help the employee improve performance. If done poorly, it can demotivate and, in some cases, destroy a person's self-confidence.

There are two types of feedback: Evaluative and developmental. *Evaluative feedback* focuses on the past and is designed to grade the employee's performance, such as in a formal performance-appraisal process. *Developmental feedback,* on the other hand, focuses on the future and is designed to help the employee raise performance or prepare for the next level of effort. For our purposes, we will limit our discussion to developmental feedback.

When giving feedback, concentrate on using "I-messages" instead of "you-messages." I-messages are statements designed to give the receiver feedback about his or her behavior. Using I-messages promotes dialogue because they reduce the other person's defensiveness and resistance to communication. You-messages that blame, accuse, or attack the other person, cause him or her to respond emotionally and negatively.

The responsibility for keeping lines of communication open rests with the coach who delivers the message honestly and focuses on behavior description, not evaluation. A behavior is something the employee does that can be observed and measured, and that can be discussed objectively. On the other hand, a discussion dealing with attitude is a conclusion one makes about an observed behavior.

Because an I-message communicates how the coach experiences the other person's behavior as well as the impact or consequences of that behavior, the employee is more likely to accept the coach's comments as positive and constructive. For example, when an employee submits reports late and full of errors, the coach might be tempted to say, "You're careless and irresponsible!" A far more effective reaction would be, "I am annoyed when you submit reports after the deadline and with errors or inaccurate information because it prevents us from finishing this project on time." Practice thinking in I-message terms by completing Action Item 7.2.

⚡ACTION ITEM 7.2 ⚡

Rewrite the following you-messages as I-messages.

"Your loan applications are always incomplete."

_____

"You don't use the proper computer settings when preparing your reports."

_____

"You aren't friendly enough with the customers."

_____

Make Feedback Immediate and Relevant

Feedback is more effective when it immediately follows performance. It should be relevant to the task and should provide the worker with information on how to improve task performance.

Keep in mind that feedback can be either positive or negative and employees often complain that the only time they receive feedback is when they do something wrong.

Practice catching people doing something right and telling them about it. Positive feedback should also be specific. It's not enough to tell a worker he or she's doing a good job and, "Keep up the good work." A much more effective and meaningful comment would be, "Maria, I liked the way you handled that difficult customer. You showed a great deal of restraint and professionalism by not raising your voice or losing control."

Feedback Guidelines

✔ *Be descriptive rather than evaluative.* Focus on behaviors that can be observed, measured, or discussed objectively, and describe them. Be careful not to put the employee on the defensive by generalizing or making assumptions. Take a look at the following statements:

"You are sloppy in your work."

"You aren't interested in helping the customers."

What's wrong with these statements? How would you react if someone said these things to you? They state personal opinion and judgment, not observable behavior. Notice how much more specific and, therefore, effective these statements are than the ones above:

"I feel frustrated when you hand in reports with incomplete, inaccurate information. I expect you to make sure you have the right information and include all the steps of the project."

"When you don't look up and acknowledge the customer in front of you, the customer may react by taking his or her business elsewhere. Because we are a customer-focused organization, I expect you to look up, smile, acknowledge the customer, and tell the customer you will be with him or her in a moment."

These two statements provide a clear model for effective feedback. They

— describe the behavior.

— describe the positive or negative consequences of that behavior.

— describe what you want.

✔ *Be specific rather than general.* Describe the behavior in the context of the actual situation. Not only should feedback describe observable behavior; it should also be stated in the context of specific incidents or situations. Useful feedback is direct, honest, and concrete.

✔ *Discuss only behavior the person can change.* Some people have shortcomings they cannot change. Or there may be circumstances or situations beyond their control, factors we will discuss in Chapter 8.

✔ *Consider both your needs and the employee's.* This approach ensures the employee's ego, self-esteem, and rights remain in tact. Remember to strive for a win-win situation.

✔ *Communicate clearly.* Check for clarity by asking the employee to state his or her understanding of the discussion. And as we noted earlier, be careful not to ask, "Do you understand?"

Encourage Employee Self-Assessment

For coaching to be effective, the employee has to buy into the process. One way to promote the collaborative aspect of coaching is to ask the employee to evaluate his or her own performance. When he or she identifies areas for improvement, he or she is more likely to make the commitment to improve.

One very good way to get people to participate is to ask the kind of open-ended questions we discussed in Chapter 5. This use of effective questioning techniques will get the employee more involved in the process and, in turn, lead to greater commitment. Open-ended questions will help you gain valuable insight into the employee's thinking. In a training situation, open-ended questions test an employee's understanding of a particular process or procedure. Open-ended coaching questions go deeper. Coaching requires a mode of questioning more oriented toward problem solving. Examples include, "What do you think is getting in the way of...?," "What have you tried to do to...?" or "How can I help you improve your...?" Asking a worker to "tell me more about..." is a powerful way to encourage someone to expand his or her comments. Questions starting with "Why" should be used with caution because they risk coming across as challenging and may cause the employee to become defensive. Take a look at Action Item 7.3 and craft some appropriate questions.

➤ ACTION ITEM 7.3 ➤

Think about the employee who needs coaching. Make a list of open-ended questions you could ask to help identify underlying problems or extenuating circumstances.

➤ _____

➤ _____

➤ _____

➤ _____

➤ _____

Actively Listen

After asking open-ended questions, the effective coach will employ active listening techniques to encourage the employee to open up even more. Many supervisors fail in their coaching efforts because they spend more of their time talking in a coaching session, _telling_ the employee how to handle the situation differently instead of asking questions and really _listening_ to the employee.

People confuse hearing with listening. Studies show that at best, we listen at only a 25 percent level of effectiveness. Hearing is physical; it happens when your ears sense sound waves. Listening, however, involves interpreting, evaluating, and reacting.

Listening is the process of taking in information from the sender or speaker without judging, clarifying what we think we heard, and responding to the speaker in a way that invites the communication to continue. Listening is one of the most important, most underused, and least understood coaching skills. If you're wondering, "How can I coach someone through listening?" consider this: How do you feel when someone *really* listens to you? You probably feel respected and appreciated. When people sense that others are listening to them and trying to understand their viewpoints, they begin to open up and drop their own barriers. The result is a climate of trust, openness, and mutual respect that leads to greater cooperation and better coaching results.

Read the coaching conversation in the sidebar below and notice how the coach/listener encourages the employee by using active listening techniques.

Coach:

What are some other ways you could have responded to the customer's objections?

  Ask an open-ended question

Employee:

I don't know. I thought I handled it correctly.

Coach:

Okay. Let's approach it another way. What is your understanding of the customer's objections?

  Another open-ended question

Employee:

The customer was only concerned about price. He kept saying that our competitor has a similar product that costs a lot less.

Coach:

Let me make sure I understand. What I hear you saying is that the customer objects only to the cost of our product.

  Confirming

Employee:

Yes, that's right.

Coach:

How did you respond to the customer?

  Another open-ended question

Employee:

I told him that our product was of much higher quality.

Coach:

If I understand you correctly, you pointed out to him the specific features of our product and how our product compared to the competition.

  Clarifying

Employee:

Well, not exactly. I just told him ours was better.

Coach:

What specific points could you have made to show that our product is better?

  Another open-ended question

Reach Meaningful Agreement

In the self-assessment step, the employee may try various ways to dodge the issue and accept no responsibility for the poor performance. In many cases, the employee agrees that a problem exists but places the blame on someone or something else. Your careful documentation will be of invaluable support, particularly in situations were an employee repeatedly makes excuses. In the coaching conversation cited in the sidebar, the employee might respond that "the customer already had his mind made up" and "it would be a waste of time to offer any further explanations." An effective coach would point out that the employee has used the same approach on more than one occasion and would further ask the employee to agree that he or she has not really pushed to convince the customer to buy our product.

Through two-way communication, you and the employee should agree that the employee is not meeting expectations and agree about the impact it has not only on the employee but also on the organization and on others. This step is critical. This is a developmental process and both parties should collaborate to identify what needs to change in order for the employee to perform at an acceptable level. It may be very tempting to lay down the law and tell the employee what he or she should do, but it's the course of last resort.

Identify Obstacles and Barriers

To help the employee identify possible barriers to success, you could ask, "What do you think is preventing you from...?" In this manner, you place the onus on the employee and make him or her take appropriate ownership. By the same token, you will want to ask what you can do to help. It may be that what the employee wants you to do is not appropriate or possible. For example, the employee may want to go back to doing the task "the old way." If that's the case, it's a good starting point for further discussion and maybe even some negotiation. The employee may offer a solution you had not considered.

Develop Solutions and Action Plans

Sometimes during coaching sessions employees bring up problems and want the supervisor to tell them how to solve them. This is often an outgrowth of the self-assessment process. It is more effective, however, if the coach helps the employee solve his or her own problem. This approach takes time and requires the mastery of certain communication skills on the part of the manager.

The problem-solving model comprises three parts: Diagnosing the problem, generating alternative action or behavior, and identifying consequences for each action.

Diagnosis: During this phase, the coach asks the employee specific questions to help identify real or perceived barriers. The question should focus on asking what he or she thinks might be the problem or obstacle.

Alternative Action or Behavior: The coach then asks questions that will help the worker think about what he or she could have done differently in the situation. These questions force the employee to view the situation from a different perspective.

Consequences of Action: The final questions focus on possible outcomes of the alternative action. In essence, the coach is asking "What if...?" questions of the employee.

Sometimes the coach will need to demonstrate the preferred actions through role playing. Much as in the initial training situation, the coach will assume the role of the employee in the scenario, and the employee will play the other person involved. For example, let's assume the employee needs some coaching in how to handle an irate customer. In a spontaneous role play, the coach will play the customer service representative and the employee will play the irate customer. In that way the coach can demonstrate the appropriate way to handle the customer. Modeling the desired behavior is far more effective than merely telling the employee what he or she should have done or should do the next time.

Get the Employee to Commit to a Plan of Action

An important part of the developmental coaching process is letting employees participate actively in goal setting. People know their own capabilities and limitations. Personal goal setting results in a commitment to goal accomplishment. The coach and employee should establish performance improvement goals that are specific, realistic, attainable, simple, and timebound as well as strategies for overcoming barriers to achieving those goals. Once again, use of good questioning techniques helps to get the employee to state what he or she plans to do to improve the performance.

Figure 7.1 Performance Improvement Plan

— What do you want to improve? Be as specific as possible.

— How will you know when you've reached your improvement goal?

— What obstacles (internal or external) may hinder your attempt to reach your goal?

— Who or what can be a source of help to you in reaching your goal or overcoming obstacles?

— What action steps will you take to accomplish your goal? Be specific.

In this step, the employee takes ownership of the problem and commits to improving performance by stating exactly what he or she is going to do to improve the situation. Once you gain agreement and commitment, ask the employee to summarize the discussion.

Figure 7.1 offers a series of questions to help you arrive at an improvement plan. Prepare the questions in written form for both you and your employee to follow during the improvement planning phase of the coaching session. It provides a way for the employee not only to take ownership but also to monitor his or her progress.

Establish Follow-up Sessions

Successful coaching requires an action plan and follow-up. You should state precisely what you want the employee to do. It's a good idea to ask the employee to summarize the session by stating what he or she is going to work on. Also, ask what you can do to support the employee in his or her efforts to improve performance.

Before concluding the coaching session, you and the employee must agree on a time to meet to discuss progress. The next meeting should be scheduled to give ample time for the employee to practice the skills or behavior but not so much that he or she assumes the matter is forgotten.

Monitor the Employee's Progress

It is vital to the performance improvement that you monitor the employee's work and give specific feedback in the form of comments, instructions, and suggestions based on your firsthand observations. You may suggest how to do something better by saying, "Next time, Sara, try asking the customer how she is going to use the account so that you can offer the appropriate choices." Another example of reinforcing positive behavior may be, "Ivan, you handled that customer well. Although you couldn't give her what she wanted, you gave her a choice and allowed her to make her own decision." Immediate praise is a powerful reinforcer. If you want the behavior repeated, you need to let the person know.

Coaching takes time, practice, and patience. To guide you through the process, remember that effective coaches practice the five Rs: Respect, reinforcement, recognition/reward, and role modeling to develop employees into peak performers and create a winning team.

Coaching gets results. The organization benefits from improved employee performance, increased productivity, and bottom-line results. The employee benefits from increased self-esteem and job satisfaction. The supervisor/coach benefits by meeting goals and objectives with less stress.

Chapter 8
Management Commitment

Chapter Objectives:

- Gain management commitment to a structured OJT process
- Develop a partnership with line managers and supervisors to identify and meet training needs
- Establish a system that recognizes and rewards successful performance
- Develop a train-the-trainer program

To improve productivity and reduce training costs, a structured OJT program should be designed to reduce turnover, improve morale, and cut training time. Management support is key to a successful program. From the very beginning, line managers and training professionals will need to work together to determine exactly what should be measured and how that measurement is tied to a business need.

Get Line Managers to Identify Training Targets

The first step is to involve the line manager or supervisor in identifying the business need that OJT can help meet. During this step, face-to-face dialogue with the line managers is very important. But don't ask them, "What are your training needs?" First, they'll probably tell you that they don't have any training needs. Training takes time, and time is in short supply in today's corporate climate. Ask, "What are your department goals? What's keeping you from reaching them?" Or, "What are your employees doing well? What are they not doing so well?" That is your hook to show them how training can help.

Training Is Not Always the Answer

In examining possible causes of a performance problem, it's important to ask, "Is it a training problem? Can training fix it?" Does the problem arise from a lack of knowledge or skill, or is it an operational problem that is not training related? For example, you may have a situation where a manager has identified employees who need training on proper telephone usage because customers calling in are being disconnected when the person who answered the phone tries to transfer their calls. If the phone system isn't set up to handle multiple functions, then all the training in the world won't solve the problem. Similarly, you may identify a customer service representative who needs training on handling customer complaints and dealing with irate customers, but the training won't solve the real problem if slow delivery makes it difficult for the customer to receive the product on time.

Overcome Resistance by Describing the Gains

Managers and supervisors may be reluctant to support a structured OJT program. They may think it's just another training fad that won't yield any significant results. Or, they may believe a structured program will take more time or cost more money. Perhaps they hold the philosophy that "if it ain't broke, you don't fix it." Things have been done "this way" for years with no big problems, so why change?

One way to overcome this opposition is to show resistant managers and supervisors how a structured OJT program can benefit them. An effective approach is to address the productivity breakdown cycle that occurs when there are deficiencies in the overall department operation. Problems left untreated escalate, causing bigger problems that may cause irreparable damage. Once this dynamic begins, it becomes difficult to identify the real cause. As a result, the breakdown cycle perpetuates itself.

For example, during a department store's annual clearance sale, a customer approaches a sales associate with a complicated exchange transaction that involves a combination of cash and credit. The associate who has had no training on unusual transactions has no idea how to process this transaction. A long line begins to form with customers eager to take advantage of the great bargains during this once-a-year sale. The sales associate goes for help from an employee at another register, but that employee is also inundated with customers and too busy to help. Meanwhile, customers at both registers are growing irritated with the poor service. The new associate tries to figure out what to do but only succeeds in making matters worse. An angry customer finally summons the supervisor who eventually straightens everything out and later reprimands the new associate for handling the situation poorly. As a result, the sales associate loses confidence in himself and his ability to learn this job. He also loses respect for the supervisor and begins to develop a negative attitude toward his supervisor, coworkers, and the entire organization. His performance suffers and he is eventually fired and replaced with a new associate. As one might imagine, the cycle repeats itself.

Training, however, can help overcome this productivity breakdown cycle. A structured on-the-job training program would prevent such scenarios from taking place. The system in place would ensure that the associate would not be sent to fend for himself on such a busy day without adequate training or a readily available support system. The sales associate would have been prepared to handle any and all types of transactions prior to working independently with customers. As a result, the customers would have received prompt, courteous service, the supervisor would not have gotten involved, and the new associate would be happy with himself and his job.

Many key decision makers believe that if the way they learned the ropes was good enough for them, it should be good enough for everyone else. That short-sightedness prevents the organization from bringing newly hired and retrained workers up to speed so they can begin to shoulder more of the work and responsibility. Even worse is the danger of those people leaving the company out of frustration because they've not been given the knowledge and skills to succeed.

Winning management support and commitment to OJT is critical. Show them the benefits. Show them that OJT is working well in other organizations. Share articles, books, and studies. Show how OJT can improve performance and in turn improve the bottom line. Establish an advisory committee of line managers and supervisors who will share their experiences with a structured OJT program and offer feedback and suggestions on how the program can be improved.

Get Managers Involved as Coaches

One of the toughest aspects of a structured OJT program is getting managers to accept their role as coaches. A successful program, however, will include components that will help supervisors and others improve and increase the use of their coaching skills. Coaching is becoming increasingly crucial as more organizations form self-directed work teams.

Once a manager understands that his or her role as coach is vital to the success of the department, you can help by offering a coaching training session and sharing the information provided in Chapter 7. It's important that the line manager understands that he or she has the ultimate responsibility for ensuring that effective training has taken place and is being applied on the job.

Strategies for Avoiding Pitfalls

Even with upper-level support, even after selecting the right person to do the job and the right person to do the training, success is not guaranteed. There are, however, practical strategies that organizations can use to avoid potential pitfalls.

A Formal Training Plan

Good training requires an organized instructional plan complete with objectives, outlines, time frames, and a procedures manual. Without a formalized plan, important details can be overlooked and consistency and uniformity will suffer.

Clearly Communicated Expectations

The manager needs to explain to the chosen trainer why he or she was selected for the extra assignment and all of the specific expectations that pertain. The manager should take a positive tack, citing specific examples of the person's qualifications for this assignment. This approach can prevent the trainer from using the training assignment as an excuse not to do other duties or from feeling overwhelmed and dumped on. Ideally, all employees should view training others as part of their routine job responsibilities.

Time for Learning and Training

The designated trainer needs time to learn *how* to train as well as time to do the training. Otherwise the organization sends the message that training really isn't so important. In making a training assignment, the manager needs to state up front that training is a top priority. The manager should ask the trainer to decide how much preparation time he or she needs, how long the actual training will take, and also how much time should be allotted to follow-up. The trainer's workload during the training period should be lightened, and this situational redistribution of duties and responsibilities helps promote teamwork. As a result, everyone in the department realizes the importance of well-trained individual team members, and they are rewarded for team performance. In short, take the time to do it right. In accordance with the basic principles of time management, one hour of planning saves three to four hours in execution.

An Attitude of Support and Reward

Recognition of the importance of training needs to be communicated throughout the organization. Management needs to allocate not only time but money for training programs, including resources and materials as well as rewards and recognition for both trainers and trainees. The training assignment can be a reward in itself, particularly in high-stress jobs. The extra effort should be noted on trainers' performance appraisals and should influence promotional decisions.

For trainees who succeed, individual recognition teamed with incentive programs can be very effective but should be tied to organizational goals and individual performance, and valued by the employee. For example, if the organization is committed to responding quickly to customers, then it should reward the employee's efficiency in returning phone calls or resolving complaints. Likewise, if the organization values training, then those people charged with additional responsibilities should be rewarded for success.

Rewards need not always be costly. Where budgets are limited and financial incentives are not available, there are options that require little or no money. The reward could be public praise, special privileges, or choices in flex-time, schedules, or vacations. Tangibles such as money, plaques, theater tickets, or other token gifts can promote good feelings and good will. They improve job satisfaction and make the trainer and trainee feel more like part of the team. Keep in mind that the reward should depend on the person receiving it. The employee with young children may appreciate being given more scheduling flexibility and someone on a limited income would value the opportunity to work overtime.

Training Follow-up

Hold regular meetings of designated trainers to discuss what works, what doesn't, and how the program can be improved. Arrange for ongoing training opportunities for designated trainers.

Invest in Train-the-Trainer Programs

Supervisors and other designated trainers should attend train-the-trainer sessions. Such programs, should not only give the participants an opportunity to learn about the active approach to OJT but should also allow them to try out or demonstrate their training skills and receive feedback from the instructor and their peers. Figure 8.1 presents a general design for a train-the-trainer program. You can use the information and activities in this book to develop your program in detail.

An investment in training will result in increased worker competence and motivation. The employee gains self-esteem and employment security. The organization benefits through increased productivity and profitability. Everybody wins.

Figure 8.1 Plan for a Train-the-Trainer Program

Program Description
Training, an ongoing process in the workplace, takes many forms, from new employee orientation to inserting new members into functioning teams. This workshop gives trainers the tools and techniques to use in developing a systematic approach to OJT.

Participants
Line managers, assistant managers, first-line supervisors, project leaders, and any individual designated to train others on the job

Time Required
Two days with lots of opportunities to practice

Learning Outcomes
Participants will learn how to…
— Identify the criteria used in selecting a potential trainer.
— Design a framework for training.
— Create the proper environment.
— Create effective training materials.
— Use feedback and reinforcement techniques.
— Measure results to ensure the transfer of training.

Topical Outline
A. Introduction
     1. Training versus teaching
     2. Active training principles
     3. Role of trainer
     4. Trainer skills and characteristics
B. Principles of Adult Learning
     1. How and why adults learn
     2. Learning styles and teaching styles
     3. Application of learning characteristics
     4. Trainee's responsibility
C. Orienting the New Employee
     1. Employee's concerns and expectations
     2. Organization orientation
     3. Department orientation
D. Basics of One-on-One Instruction
     1. Identify training needs
     2. Barriers to learning
     3. Framework for training
        a. Job/task analysis
        b. Training plan
     4. Conducting training
        a. Process
        b. Skills
E. Techniques for Effective Learning
     1. The power of pairs
     2. Using active training techniques
     3. Using training aids and visuals
F. Evaluation and Follow-up
     1. Evaluating employee's performance
     2. Evaluating trainer's performance
     3. Evaluating program success
     4. Ensuring transfer of training
     5. Measuring results

Chapter 9
Orienting the New Employee

Chapter Objectives:
- ‣ Identify the universal concerns of new employees
- ‣ Develop pleasant, memorable, and productive orientation programs at both department and organization levels for the new employee

New employees are filled with anxiety and confusion. They're overwhelmed. As soon as they accept a position they begin to question the decision they've made. Did I do the right thing? Am I really qualified to do this job? Will I like my boss and the people I work with? Will I fit in? The way in which a person is treated on his or her first day will determine if those fears and anxieties were warranted, and as a result, how he or she will approach this new experience.

VIGNETTE 9.1 THE UNPRODUCTIVE ORIENTATION

*S*usan arrived at the office 15 minutes early, anxious to begin her new job. *From her interviewing experience, she knew she was going to like working here. She opened the door and entered the reception area. Empty. After waiting 10 minutes, she started to wander beyond the reception area, hoping to find someone to tell her where to go and what to do. Finally a voice came from behind a partition: "Can I help you?"*

"I'm looking for Mr. Wallace."

"Why? What do you want to see him for? Who are you?"

"I'm Susan Winkler and I'm a new employee."

"Nobody told us anything about a new employee. Just a minute. I'll see what I can find out." For five minutes Susan stood waiting in the hall.

Finally the person returned. "Mr. Wallace won't be in until this afternoon. What job are you here for?"

"I'm the new accounts receivable clerk."

"Nobody was expecting you, but I'll put you in Joan's office since she's on vacation. When Mr. Wallace comes in he can tell you what to do. Until then, here's our policy manual for you to read."

The rest of the day was much the same. Lunchtime came and Susan had to ask where she could get something to eat. She stopped a woman in the hall to ask directions to the restroom. After eating alone, she returned to her assigned spot to wait for Mr. Wallace. The afternoon wore on, and Mr. Wallace never appeared. At five o'clock, Susan took her coat from the chair and left. She would not return.

Read the first-day vignette on the previous page. Does the situation sound familiar? Exaggerated? Every day new employees are introduced to their jobs in similar fashions. Unlike Susan, many come back the next day but they already have a negative attitude about the company, the boss, and their coworkers.

OJT Begins on Day One

The new employee needs to feel comfortable in his or her new surroundings, whether the employee is an executive or an entry-level clerk, new to the company or just to a department. Comfort level should be a primary consideration and it's the manager's or supervisor's responsibility to expedite the employee's adapting to the work environment. The first step in a successful on-the-job training program is the orientation process, and communication is the key.

In a global sense, the purpose of an orientation program is to provide information, share ideas, and establish mutual trust from the beginning. Specifically, it should be designed to (a) promote two-way communication, (b) reduce anxiety, (c) promote a positive employee attitude, and (d) assimilate the employee into the organization.

Orienting the new employee goes beyond the company's formal orientation program. The first day is critical to the employee's success and for that reason should be carefully planned and orchestrated. As managers and supervisors, we need to handle the basics, help the employee adjust quickly so he can concentrate on doing what he was hired to do. Failure to orient the employee properly will result in poor attitude, low morale and productivity, performance problems, and in some cases the loss of a valuable worker. The sooner an employee adapts and feels comfortable, the sooner she becomes productive. Even before the employee arrives at the workarea, efforts should be underway to help him feel a part of the team and the organization.

Let's consider the employee's immediate needs and concerns. Put yourself in that person's shoes. Think back to your first day on the job. How did you feel? What were your concerns and expectations? What did you want and need to know? Take a look at the list of first-day queries below. Identifying what the newly hired worker needs and wants to know to survive the first few days is a critical place to start. A manager or supervisor will be on target in addressing the new employee's concerns if he or she approaches orientation from the basic who, what, where, when, why, and how questions.

WHERE
✔ Where will I find…?
— restrooms
— lunch area
— my work area
— employee lounge
— supplies
— equipment
— reference material
— files and records

✔ Where should I park?

HOW
✔ How do I operate the…?
— telephone
— photocopier
— facsimile machine
— postage meter
— computer or word processor

✔ How do I fit into this department?

✔ How will I be evaluated?

✔ How will I be compensated for
overtime?

✔ How do I process the mail?

✔ How do I order supplies?

WHO

✔ Who is senior management?

✔ Who can I go to for help?

✔ Who do I report to?

✔ Who do I interact with?

WHEN

✔ When do I go to lunch and take
breaks?

✔ When will I be paid?

✔ When will I be evaluated?

✔ When should I report for work
each day?

✔ When can I expect to leave each
day?

WHAT

✔ What are the job requirements?

✔ What are the manager's expectations?

✔ What are the standards of performance?

✔ What are the policies and procedures regarding…?
— coffee pot
— lunch room clean-up
— smoking
— dress
— sickness
— vacation
— parties
— call-in
— travel and expense reports

✔ What is the structure of the
department?

WHY

✔ Why do we follow that
procedure?

✔ Why do I have to do this?

In addition to basic information, new employees also have certain wants and expectations. They want to be treated like people. They want to know what is expected of them
and how they will go about learning their new jobs. They want to know how they will be
rewarded and how they fit into the total picture. We tend to overlook or forget that people begin a job with success in mind; they genuinely want to do well. This commitment
and enthusiasm is either squelched or encouraged within the first few hours on the job.

Departmental Employee Orientation

Welcoming and assimilating a new worker begins before that person's first day. To prepare for the new employee's arrival, do the following things:

➡ Inform the staff that a new employee will be joining the department. Tell them when
the employee will arrive, what he or she will be doing, where he or she will be located, and share some information about the employee such as previous job, background, and qualifications.

➡ Prepare the employee's workarea, making certain that all needed supplies, manuals, forms, and directories are available and that all equipment is in working order.

➡ Select a department member to be the newcomer's mentor. It will be that person's responsibility to show the new employee around, make introductions, answer questions, and help make him or her feel welcome and a part of the group. The person selected should have many of the same qualities as a designated trainer. In fact, the mentor and the trainer could be the same person. The advantage of using two different people is that the new employee will be exposed to more people in different relationships and situations.

➡ Review the information to be covered with the employee on the first day.

The First Day

In most companies the employee will report first to the human resources department for employment processing. She'll receive benefits information, sign the necessary employment processing forms, and be given an employee handbook outlining the company's policies and procedures.

About midmorning, the employee will leave the human resources department to report to her worksite. The supervisor should greet the new employee personally and set aside adequate time to introduce her to the work environment.

First-day orientation is not something a supervisor should delegate. It's too important. This initial interaction establishes lines of communication between the supervisor and new employee. The supervisor's responsibility is to set the tone and create a climate that helps reduce the employee's anxiety. Their relationship is critical to the employee's success on the job.

The supervisor should begin by getting acquainted with the employee, relating on a personal level. Ask questions about the family and how the employee feels about starting a new job. The next step is to review the job duties and responsibilities, performance expectations and standards, and company policies such as sick time, vacations, hours, pay, dress code, overtime, smoking policy, and corporate customs. In addition, the employee should receive a departmental information packet containing an organizational chart, department and organization telephone directory, manuals, safety rules, health regulations, and other useful materials such as company brochures, the employee newsletter, annual report, and list of resource people. To ensure uniformity and consistency, the supervisor should prepare a checklist of topics to be addressed during the orientation period. Be sure to give a copy to the new employee so he or she will know what to expect. Since the organization orientation will cover personnel policies and practices as well as a more global view of the organization as a whole, this particular checklist should address items peculiar to the department and the person's specific job.

An important and often overlooked area is an explanation of the unwritten practices within the department itself, the social norms such as kitchen clean-up, coffee pot, birthdays, parties, and other accepted behavior peculiar to that department. Failure to do so can result in a near-disaster. One new employee helped herself to the last cup of coffee and because it was the end of the day, she washed both the pot and cup and put them back in place. The next morning one of her coworkers asked, "Did you drink the last cup of coffee yesterday?" Without waiting for an answer, she said bitterly, "Around here, the person who empties the pot is responsible for making a fresh one. Don't let it happen again." The new employee was hurt and embarrassed and went out of her way to avoid any further contact with the coworker. Such a humiliating experience could have been avoided if the supervisor had just taken a minute to explain the department's practice.

Unwritten customs should be communicated to everyone new to the department—not just those new to the company. People who've been with the organization for a while and are transferred to a new department are often overlooked. Remember that this is a totally new environment for that employee as well.

Look at Action Item 9.1 below and think about your department. What specific information would you need to tell the new employee?

➤ ACTION ITEM 9.1 ➤

Take a moment and prepare a checklist of the basic topics or areas you need to address during an employee's orientation period. For the sake of this activity, just list the major topics. You can fill in the details or subtopics later.

_____

_____

_____

_____

_____

_____

_____

_____

With the preliminaries out of the way, the supervisor should begin acclimating the newcomer to the workarea itself by allowing a few minutes for settling into the workspace. Then tour the department with the new employee, introducing him to coworkers, and pointing out the locations of restrooms, supply areas, lunch facilities, the photocopy machine, bulletin boards, the mail room, and adjacent departments. At this point, it's appropriate to introduce the mentor and leave them to get acquainted. This get-acquainted process will be helped by having the mentor explain how to operate the telephone system and other equipment or how to order supplies. The mentor should also accompany the newcomer to lunch, and introduce him to others in the organization.

At the end of the day, the supervisor should meet once again with the new worker to answer any questions, review important information, give encouragement, and reinforce how pleased everyone in the department is to have this employee on the team.

The Second Day

On the second day, the OJT process should begin with the trainer greeting the new worker first thing in the morning. As discussed in the previous chapters, the OJT should be structured and designed to get the employee working comfortably and independently as soon as possible. The employee's mentor should remain in the picture, arranging to go on breaks and lunches together and offering support.

The First Week

At the end of the first week, the manager should meet with the employee once again to check on progress, answer questions, and provide additional information such as department goals and objectives, the performance planning and evaluation process, and career development opportunities. At this point, the manager may also want to review the company's mission statement and goals and explain how the department and the individual fit into the total organization. If it seems more appropriate, delay an in-depth discussion of the big picture until after the employee's initial adjustment period when it might be more relevant and meaningful. If an organization-level orientation is planned, the manager may omit discussing the goals and mission and leave that to the later session.

Organization-Level Employee Orientation

Within four to six weeks, the employee should attend an organization-level orientation that addresses the company's history, its philosophy and culture, and its goals and direction. The purpose is to introduce the employee to the company as a whole and help him feel a part of it. This is also a good opportunity to elaborate on career opportunities and emphasize the importance of each person's contribution to the success of the organization. Members of senior management should participate as guest speakers, preferably in person or at the very least on videotape. A nice touch is to host a short reception either during a break or after the session during which members of management mingle with the newcomers, getting to know them on a personal level and answering any questions they were hesitant to ask in front of the group. Depending on the size of the organization, "Breakfast with the President" might be another element of the orientation process in which the president or another senior manager meets with a group of new employees who've been on the job about three months. Over rolls and coffee the senior member solicits feedback and answers questions that employees have about the organization as a whole. This is a good opportunity to identify and address potential problems before they become major issues and to help remove some of the mystique employees often ascribe to senior management.

The following checklist of topics to address may be helpful in structuring an organization orientation:

➡ Products and services

➡ Organizational structure

➡ Senior management team and department heads

➡ Company history

➡ Corporate philosophy and values

➡ Mission statement

➡ Goals and direction

➡ Organizational profile

➡ Policies

➡ Financial position

➡ Customers

➡ Competition

➡ Code of ethics

There are some very creative ways you can cover the important topics listed above. Taking a cue from the design of OJT programs where active learning is more useful than mere watching or listening, try some of the following activities to make your organization-level orientation come alive (Silberman and Lawson 1995).

Information Round-Robin
➡ Several weeks before the orientation session, invite key members of each department or division to serve as roundtable leaders. These should be people at a relatively high level within the company, such as directors or vice presidents.

➡ Ask them to prepare a five- or 10-minute overview of their division that they will deliver during several rounds of discussion. They should also be prepared to solicit questions from the new employees during each round.

➡ On orientation day, form several small groups. Participants will remain with their respective groups for each round of discussion.

➡ At each round, subgroups move to a table to meet and speak with one or another department representative.

Panel Discussion
➡ Prior to the orientation session, ask five or six members of various departments to participate as panel members. These people should be fairly new—less than two years with the company.

➡ Ask them to prepare brief (no more than five-minute) answers to the following questions:

What do you wish you had been told as a new employee?

What is your most memorable experience as a new employee?

➡ During the orientation session, after each panelist has presented his or her remarks, the panel moderator will invite questions from the group of new employees.

"Press" Conference

➡ Invite one or two key people in the company (CEO, CFO, COO) to address a group of new employees.

➡ Explain to the guest speaker(s) that part of the session will be conducted like a press conference where the speaker presents some brief remarks or opening statement and then answers questions from "the press," that is, the employees.

➡ Prior to the speaker's appearance, prepare the participants by explaining the format of the session and asking them to prepare several questions to ask the speaker. If you think participants will be reluctant to ask questions directly, distribute index cards and ask participants to write down their questions. You can then collect them, quickly categorize (and screen) them, and give them to the speaker to answer.

Company Scavenger Hunt

➡ A week or so prior to the session, send a memo to all departments explaining that during the company's orientation session, group members will be participating in a scavenger hunt and will be visiting different areas of the company to collect items and information. Give a specific time frame when they can expect the visitors and ask for each department's cooperation. Be sure you have the permission of each area before you conduct the activity.

➡ On orientation day, subdivide participants into groups of three.

➡ Explain that they will be moving throughout the building in teams of three, collecting information and items from various areas of the company.

➡ Give them a time limit and tell them to be as quiet, respectful, and nonintrusive as possible.

➡ Distribute a list of 10 to 12 items to locate and bring back to the meeting room. The following are just a few suggestions of what you might want to include:

Business card from a specific department or person.

Sample product that the company makes.

Color or pattern of the drapes in someone's office or an area of the building.

Number of wall hangings in a specific area.

A form from a particular department.

➡ Award prizes to the group that finishes first.

➡ Complete the process by discussing what they discovered and how the activity has helped them learn more about the company.

Information Search

➡ Put participants into groups of three or four and give each subgroup a set of written company materials, such as product brochures, employee handbook, and annual report.

➡ Also distribute to each subgroup a worksheet with questions about the company, its history, products, and personnel policies. Suggested questions may include the following:

> Who is the CEO of the company?
> When was the company founded?
> How many divisions does the company have?
> How many employees does the company have?
> How many paid holidays do employees get?
> What is the company's primary product?
> What is the name of the company newsletter?
> When are performance appraisals given?
> Instruct subgroups to complete the worksheet by searching the packet of materials for the information. Be sure to give a time limit.

➡ Award a prize to the subgroup that finishes first or gets all the answers correct.

➡ Process the activity by reforming the larger group and discussing the information gained.

Ice Breakers

Ideally, the orientation should not only provide an opportunity for the new employee to learn significant details about the organization. It should also be conducted in a manner that reflects adult learning principles and incorporates active training practices. For starters, kick off the formal orientation session with an activity designed to create a comfortable environment and get people mixing and mingling quickly. Please! Don't use the tired old standby of going around the room and asking each person to do a self-introduction. It's boring, predictable, and awkward. After the first five or six people, no one is paying attention. Here are a couple of creative, fun, and energizing get-acquainted activities.

Human Scavenger Hunt

No matter how many times people participate in this activity, every time is different and people love it.

➡ Create a handout with a list of descriptive statements to complete the phrase, "Find someone in this group who…." The statements might include any of the following:

lives less than 30 miles from work
has worked for one of our competitors
has worked in an entirely different business or industry
has more than two children
was born in the same month as you
enjoys working with people
has more than two pets
belongs to a professional organization
enjoys the same type of music as you
has a friend or relative working in the organization
recently graduated from high school or college.

➡ Distribute the handouts and ask participants to circulate around the room and find people who meet the various criteria. When they make a connection, they are to ask that person to sign his or her name next to the item. Tell them they may not have any one person sign in more than one space and then give them a time limit.

➡ Call time, award a prize to the person(s) who completed their sheets or who had the most spaces filled.

➡ Conduct a brief discussion of some of the more interesting items by asking people to tell a little more about themselves through a particular criterion they may have met. For example, you might ask, "Who worked for one of our competitors?" When someone puts up his or her hand, you might ask that person to tell the group who he or she worked for and what the person liked about the other organization.

Finding Famous Fictional Friends and Families

➡ Identify groups of fictional characters from television, movies, or cartoons (*Peter Pan, M.A.S.H., Star Wars, Superman,* etc.) and list four or five characters for each (e.g., Peter Pan, Captain Hook, Wendy, Tinkerbell).

➡ Put each character name on a separate index card. Create as many cards as there are people in your orientation group.

➡ Shuffle the cards and distribute one to each group member and ask them not to reveal their new identity.

➡ Tell them that when you give the signal, they are to get up, mingle, and find the rest of their fictional family, choose a spot to congregate, and await further instructions.

➡ Once the groups have formed, ask them to do any or all of the following:
—Briefly introduce themselves by stating their true name (not the one on the index card) and what department or area they will be working in.
—Identify things the group members have in common.
—State one thing he or she wants to know about the company.

—Tells why he or she joined the company.

—Be sure to give the groups a time limit and ask each group to designate a scribe or a spokesperson. If possible, ask the groups to capture information, such as the things they have in common or what they want to know on flipchart paper, and post these sheets around the room.

—If time allows, you may want to have more than one round by shuffling the cards and redistributing them so that people will form new groups. Each round should have a different primary question. Repeating the process will create more opportunities for group members to meet more people.

Quality Control

In order for the orientation process to be successful, it must be established as a formal program with a program administrator. Although the responsibility for orientation often falls to the human resources department, any department can handle it. The training department, for example, can be very helpful by conducting orientation training sessions for managers and supervisors. These sessions should include the following:

➡ The purpose and objectives of an orientation program

➡ The importance of orientation and its impact on performance and turnover

➡ The supervisor's/manager's role

➡ The benefits of proper orientation for the employee, the supervisor, and the company

➡ Checklists and manuals to help guide managers and supervisors through the orientation process

➡ Follow-up procedures.

Follow-up to the Orientation

Follow-up is an important part of a successful program. The orientation administrator should establish a feedback system by surveying new employees about the effectiveness of the program and asking managers and supervisors for suggestions to improve and enhance the program.

Successful orientation is a joint effort between the organization and the employee. To promote this two-way responsibility, provide each new employee with an orientation workbook designed to make them proactive participants in their orientation and to take job ownership from day one of their employment.

References

American Society for Training and Development. 1988. *Workplace Basics: The Skills Employers Want.* Alexandria, Va.: American Society for Training and Development.

Barron, J.M., D.A. Black, and M.A. Lowenstein. 1989. Job Matching and On-the-Job Training. *Journal of Labor Economics* 7(11): 1-6.

Briscoe, D. 1995. Study: U.S. Schools Failing Workforce. *Philadelphia Inquirer,* July 5, p. 2.

Carnevale, A.P. and L.J. Gainer. 1989. *The Learning Enterprise.* Alexandria, Va.: American Society for Training and Development and Training Administration, U.S. Department of Labor.

Cross, P. 1980. *Adults as Learners.* San Francisco: Jossey-Bass Publishers.

Galagan, Patricia. 1994. Reinventing the Profession. *Training&Development* (December): 20-27.

Green, Ronald. 1984. The Persuasive Properties of Color. *Marketing Communications* (October): 50-54.

Jacobs, Ronald L., and Michael J. Jones. 1995. *Structured On-the-Job Training: Unleashing Employee Expertise in the Workplace.* San Francisco: Berrett-Koehler Publishers.

James, W.B. and M.W. Galbraith. 1985. Perceptual Learning Styles, Implications and Techniques for the Practitioner. *Lifelong Learning* (January): 20-23.

Johnson, David W., Roger T. Johnson, and Karl A. Smith. 1991. *Cooperative Learning: Increasing College Faculty Instructional Productivity.* ASHE-ERIC Higher Education Report No. 4. Washington, D.C.: George Washington University, School of Education and Human Development.

Kirkpatrick, Donald. 1994. *Evaluating Training Programs: The Four Levels.* San Francisco: Berrett-Koehler Publishers.

Knowles, Malcolm. 1990. *The Adult Learner: A Neglected Species.* 4th ed. Houston: Gulf Publishing Company.

Kolb, David. 1981. *Learning Style Inventory.* Boston: McBer & Company.

Lawson, Karen. 1994. On-the-Job Training: A Structured Approach. In *Twenty Active Training Programs,* Vol. II: 31-57. Edited by Mel Silberman. San Diego: Pfeiffer & Company.

Maslow, A. 1968. Defense and Growth. *Toward a Psychology of Being.* New York: Litton Educational Publishing.

McClusky, Howard. 1970. A Different Psychology of the Adult Potential. In *Adult Learning and Instruction: 80-95. Edited by Stanley M. Grabowski. Syracuse: ERIC Clearinghouse on Adult Education.*

McCord, A. 1987. "Job Training."In *Training and Development Handbook: A Guide to Human Resource Development*, edited by R. Craig. 3rd ed. New York: McGraw-Hill.

McLagan, Patricia. 1989. *Models for HRD Practice.* Alexandria, Va.: American Society for Training and Development.

Meyers, Chet and Thomas B. Jones. 1993. *Promoting Active Learning: Strategies for the College Classroom.* San Francisco: Jossey-Bass Publishers.

1995 Industry Report. 1995. *Training* (October).

Robinson, Dana Gaines and James C. Robinson. 1989. *Training for Impact.* San Francisco: Jossey-Bass Publishers.

Rothwell, W., and H.C. Kazanas. 1990. "Structured On-the-Job Training (SOJT) as Perceived by HRD Professionals." *In Performance Improvement Quarterly.* 4:12.

Silberman, Mel. 1990. *Active Training: A Handbook of Techniques, Designs, Case Examples, and Tips.* Lexington, Mass.: Lexington Books.

Silberman, Mel and Karen Lawson. 1995. *101 Ways to Make Training Active.* San Diego: Pfeiffer & Company.

Tomkins, S. 1970. Affect as the Primary Motivational System. In *Feelings and Emotions.* Edited by M.B. Arnold. New York: Academic Press.

Vella, Jane. 1994. *Learning to Listen, Learning to Teach.* San Francisco: Jossey-Bass Publishers.

Vogel, D.R., G.W. Dickson, J. Lehman, and K. Stuart. 1986. *Persuasion and the Role of Visual Presentation Support: The UM/3M Study.* Minneapolis: University of Minnesota.

Whitmore, William J. 1992. "Transferring Tecknowledgy." In *Technical & Skills Training,* (November/December): 6-9.

Wlodkowski, Raymond J. 1993. *Enhancing Adult Motivation to Learn.* San Francisco: Jossey-Bass Publishers.